FATAL DISTRACTIONS

Fatal Distractions
© 2004 Edwin B. Young
Reprinted March 2006

Published by Serendipity House Publishers
Nashville, Tennessee

In cooperation with Fellowship Church Resources
Dallas, Texas

ISBN: 1-5749-4169-0

Dewey Decimal Classification: 155.2
Subject Headings:
CHARACTER \ SIN \ TEMPTATION

1-800-525-9563
www.SerendipityHouse.com

www.fellowshipchurch.com

Printed in the United States of America
11 10 09 08 07 06   3 4 5 6 7 8 9 10

CONTENTS

HOW TO USE THIS BOOK

Small groups are a vital part of how we do ministry at Fellowship Church just as they are in many churches around the world. There are a number of different theories on how small groups should work, and they are all great in different ways. The book you are holding is written with our model in mind. So take a minute to read the following explanation, then feel free to adapt as necessary.

Each of our small groups practices a three-part agenda in every meeting. That agenda includes a social time, a discussion time, and a prayer time. Each of these elements share equal importance, but not necessarily equal time. To help you get the most out of this book, we have included an explanation of each of the parts.

The first element of every small-group meeting should be a time of socializing. This phase of the meeting should be about 30% of your time together. Welcome everyone as they arrive at the host home; make visitors feel welcome by introducing yourself and showing genuine interest in them. Enjoy some snacks, or if your group prefers, a meal together. Then move on to the second part of the meeting—the lesson.

The lesson itself may take as much as 50% of your group's meeting time. You may want to start this phase with a short "icebreaker" to get everyone talking. The questions in the "Start It Up" section of each session are what we refer to as "level the playing field" questions that everyone can participate in, regardless of their level of spiritual maturity or Bible knowledge. As your group moves through the "Talk It Up" section in each meeting, remember that it is more important to finish on time than to finish each question. It is okay to skip some questions to allow enough time to take care of the third phase of your small-group time: "Lift It Up."

The "Lift It Up" section is a vital part of every small-group meeting and should take about 20% of your time. You will be able to share with the group what God is doing in your life as well as asking the group to support you in specific prayers. To help focus this time, there are one or two questions that will prompt prayers based on the material you just covered. There is also a space for you to write down your prayer requests so you don't forget them and so you can communicate them clearly when it is your turn. Below that is a place to write down the prayer requests of the people in your group so you can remember to pray for each request throughout the week.

As an additional tool to assist you in your spiritual development journey, 10 devotionals lead up to each of the Sessions 2 through 8. Ten devotionals are provided to accommodate groups that meet every other week, giving material for five days per week during that two-week interval. If you meet weekly, ask your group members to choose at least five devotionals each week. These will help you develop a daily quiet time with God. To get the absolute most from this book, I challenge you to take 5 or 10 minutes a day to read and apply these devotionals in your life.

God's best!
Ed

FATAL DISTRACTIONS

From the green phantom fangs of envy to the one-way ego trips of pride to the atomic explosions of anger, the results of sin are real and present in each of our lives. But sin is such an ugly word. It's one of those terms that we don't like to bring out in the light. We want to cover it up and pretend that it doesn't exist, because admitting sin means admitting that we've messed up. We don't like to hear about it, talk about it, or think about it. So we've replaced it instead with words like "disease," "disorder," or "dysfunction."

From twentieth century psychologists to self-help gurus on talk shows, the message we receive today is, "I'm okay and you're okay. We aren't really to blame for our actions." Behavior, they say, is a matter of habit, not a matter of the heart.

The presence of real evil, a sinister spiritual force wreaking havoc in the world, is rarely, if ever, mentioned. We're told that people engage in "destructive behavior" because of "environmental factors." Maybe they were raised in a dysfunctional family—their parents were alcoholics or their nursery was painted the wrong color. Or perhaps it's because we're all part of one big dysfunctional society—the arts, media, schools, and government are to blame.

But the truth of the matter is that people do bad things, they sin, as a result of evil in the world and in their hearts. That's why, over the next several weeks, we're going to expose evil for what it is and take an in-depth look at some of life's most deadly sins—pride, anger, envy, lust, slothfulness, greed, and gluttony. Through this potentially life-changing study, my prayer is that we learn how to recognize and overcome each of these seven Fatal Distractions.

Make no mistake … you are going to sin. I am going to sin. After all, we're imperfect human beings. But through the power of God, as we apply His Word to our lives, we can avoid the destructive, downward spiral of sin and live above the level of life's Fatal Distractions.

Off with the Old, On with the New

Ephesians 4:22-24; Colossians 3:1-17; James 5:13-16

The Bible says that when we give our lives to Jesus, we become part of God's family and we're made into new people. So, that means the way we think and act and feel should all change, right? Daily life continues, but all is now sweetness and light. Wait just a minute. Did you just say that isn't really quite the way you've experienced it? Do you mean that Christ-followers still have to deal with sin?

If we look at ourselves honestly, we will all have to say "yes." Sin is still there, it is still a problem, and it still distracts us from following Christ. We keep doing the same old things over and over and over again. In frustration, we wonder why God hasn't magically transformed us to be sin-free, mistake-free, and problem-free. After all, that's what being a Christ-follower is all about isn't it? "The perfect life is yours if you believe in Jesus—no struggles, no pain, no sin." Then we find out this just isn't true. The struggles are still there, and it seems like nothing has really changed.

To understand our struggles, we need to look at them from a different angle. Jesus described entering God's family in an interesting way. He called it being "born again." When this happens, we are given a whole new nature. We become children of God, and we are given the Holy Spirit as our helper. But just as a baby is born into the world not yet fully mature, the new Christ-follower is "born again" as a spiritual infant. God doesn't just zap us with maturity. We have to grow up.

That's what this series is all about—growing up as Christ-followers. We still have sin problems, we still have struggles, but God doesn't say, "That's okay, I don't really care. As long as you believe in Jesus everything is fine." He wants us to work our spiritual muscles and grow in the faith. He wants us to become mature. God doesn't zap us to make us sin-free. He exercises and strengthens us to become sin-resistant and to overcome "fatal distractions."

START IT UP

Our goal is to become more like Jesus Christ. But it's an ongoing process. Most things in life require ongoing struggle and development.

1. What did you work the hardest to learn when you were growing up? Sports? Music lessons? Academics? What did you find the most rewarding?

2. Who was the hero or role model you most looked up to—someone who inspired you to really put your heart into what you were doing?

TALK IT UP

Changing Our Clothes

During Jesus' earthly ministry, He healed people with the socially and physically debilitating disease of leprosy. Even though He took care of the disease and they were completely healed, the former lepers still had to go to the priest and be cleansed (see Luke 5:14 and 17:14). They still had to take off the filthy, infected clothing that covered them. Jesus did the miracle, but they had to follow through.

Read Ephesians 4:22-24

Our lives are a lot like those lepers' lives. We are diseased spiritually. We are covered in sores, and we reek of infection. When we turn to Jesus and ask Him to take charge of our lives, He heals our diseased souls. The running sores, the infection, and the stench are all taken care of. But then He says to us, "Now take off the filthy clothes. Take off the old patterns of sin, the stinky rags you are used to wearing, and try on My kind of clothes."

Off with the Old

Read Colossians 3:1-11

Paul gives us a potent reason for changing the way we live our lives—we have been raised to life with Christ. The old person has died. There is no turning back. We belong to God, irrevocably. Because of this change, we have to destroy the remnants of the old nature. We are made new, but we are still wearing the dirty clothes. We still have habits of sin and patterns of destructive behavior that linger on. We can't wear filthy rags when we are "hidden with Christ in God" (verse 3).

3. What does the phrase "Christ, who is your life" (verse 4) mean? In what way is Christ your life?

4. What are some examples of "things above" to set your mind on (verse 2)? How real do these things seem to you?

Paul doesn't just say, "Back off from this behavior." He says, "Kill it. Destroy it. There is no room for this here." And then he gives a brief list of the kinds of behaviors he is talking about. Most of us are all too familiar with more than one item on this list. We know them well because we used to "walk in these ways" (verse 7). Even if we aren't still wearing some of these old behaviors, we are still guilty because at least some of them have been a part of our lives at some point, and no doubt we still struggle with these issues from time to time.

5. Practically speaking, how can you "put to death" the behaviors that belong to the old nature? What can you do to break old patterns and habits? Be specific.

Back in the Middle Ages a group of theologians came up with a list of what they called the Seven Mortal Sins (or Seven Deadly Sins). They were especially concerned with those attitudes and character traits that deaden our relationship with God and destroy our potential to be effective followers of Christ. While this list does not appear in the Bible as such, Scripture does teach that every one of these sins can cause serious spiritual decay. These are sins that damage our relationship with God and cut us off from His blessings. Over the next few weeks, we are going to be taking a deeper look at each one of the following Seven Deadly Sins:

Pride   Anger   Envy   Slothfulness   Lust   Gluttony   Greed

6.   Pick out one of these sins and give a specific example of how it can destroy our potential to effectively follow Christ.

The scary thing about these sins is the way they masquerade as something else in our lives. We may look at the list above and say, "Yuck! I don't behave that way!" But take a look at the following paraphrased version of the Seven Deadly Sins:

Self-confident   Resolute   Laid-back   Red-blooded   Gourmet   Ambitious

These look a little more familiar, don't they? This is not to say that all the things on this list are evil. In fact, they can be good, and that is the very reason they make such harmless-looking cloaks for the Seven Deadly Sins. God is serious when He tells us to get rid of these. They are fatal distractions—keeping our attention on self and away from the most important things of God—and they lead to death.

On with the New

Jesus gave His disciples a very important lesson. He said, "When an evil spirit comes out of a man, it goes through arid places seeking rest and does not find it. Then it says, 'I will return to the house I left.' When it arrives, it finds the house swept clean and put in order. Then it goes and takes seven other spirits more wicked than itself, and they go in and live there. And the final condition of that man is worse than the first" (Luke 11:24-26). An empty house won't stay empty long. If not filled with the Spirit of God, it will be filled with something else. In other words, we can't "take off the old" for good without putting on the new garments from God's Holy Spirit. This is worse than futile if we have not submitted to Christ.

To successfully "take off" the old way of life, we must replace bad behavior with good. More importantly, we must replace self-focus with a God-focus and an others-focus. There is no point in taking off the old if we don't put on the new. It would be like trying to sweep shadows from a room before switching on the lamp.

7. If you are comfortable, can you share a time when you thought you had swept your life clean of a sin or problem, only to have it come back later and even stronger?

Read Colossians 3:12-17

Clothing ourselves with Christ-likeness is a continuous process. Every day we put on God's designer clothing, and we have to resist the lure to add the dirty socks from our old outfit. It's a constant battle, but there is good news. The longer we wear the new clothes, the better we like them. The old clothes will seem filthier and more disgusting every time we see them. We will be eager to run to God for a spiritual bath. The Bible gives us another clue to help us keep the right spiritual clothes on: Romans 13:14 says that we need to actually "clothe [ourselves] with the Lord Jesus Christ." Jesus lives in all His followers, so as we learn to let His life and purposes rule us, His life will shine through us.

8. Compare the list of virtues in Colossians 3:12-14 with the list of sins in verses 5-9. How do these virtues counteract the vices of the first list?

9. What does it mean to "let the word of Christ dwell in you richly" (Colossians 3:16)? How can we do this, and what will it accomplish in our lives?

LIFT IT UP

Read James 5:13-16

Exercising spiritual muscles and resisting sin is hard; sometimes even painful or discouraging. Sometimes we will fail. But when we do, we must remember that God is merciful and gracious. When we confess our sins, He freely forgives (see 1 John 1:9). One of the most important weapons He has given in our battle is friends. By praying for, encouraging, and loving each other, we can be props of strength.

10. How can we show love to one another in this group? Share practical ideas and prayer requests so that you may be healed and happy.

11. Do you have the Spirit of God at work in your life? If you are not sure, the leader of the group will be glad to talk to you and help you.

Take time to pray specifically for each other in areas where you need the Spirit's help to overcome sin. Remember to include the prayer requests from question #10.

My Prayer Needs:

_____

_____

_____

_____

My Group's Prayer Needs:

_____

_____

_____

_____

_____

_____

_____

_____

DEVOTIONALS

DAY 1

Out of the Shadows

This is the verdict: Light has come into the world, but men loved darkness instead of light because their deeds were evil. Everyone who does evil hates the light and will not come into the light for fear that his deeds will be exposed. But whoever lives by the truth comes into the light, so that it may be seen plainly that what he has done has been done through God (John 3:19-21).

Jesus Christ is the "Light" that "has come into the world." Evildoers hate light, because light exposes the true nature of their deeds. For the same reason, when we do evil deeds and are living in sin, we don't feel comfortable in the presence of Christ. His Light shows us for what we really are. However, when we become Christ-followers, we suddenly start seeing ourselves in a way we have never seen ourselves before. When we are walking in darkness, it is easy to overlook our ragged clothes, the stains and filth, the wrong thoughts and actions. The shadows hide our sins and we don't have to look at them. When we walk with Christ, we are out in the daylight, measuring ourselves against truth. How do our actions and thoughts measure up to the truth? Can they stand the light of day and the Light of Jesus?

Take a good look at yourself, and your relationship with Christ. Are you walking in the light, willing to have Jesus expose your sins and help you deal with them, or are you trying to follow Him but staying back in the shadows so your rags of sin won't show? Which one of the Seven Deadly Sins or "fatal distractions" do you most need Jesus' help with today?

DAY 2

New Clothes

The night is nearly over; the day is almost here. So let us put aside the deeds of darkness and put on the armor of light. Let us behave decently, as in the daytime, not in orgies and drunkenness, not in sexual immorality and debauchery, not in dissension and jealousy. Rather, clothe yourselves with the Lord Jesus Christ, and do not think about how to gratify the desires of the sinful nature (Romans 13:12-14).

When we become Christ-followers, we have exchanged worlds. Instead of belonging to the darkness of the lost world, we belong to eternity. Our real home is the "day" of life with Christ, not the "night" of this world. We have to learn to make our behavior match our real home. The old rags of sinful behavior don't fit in. They are filthy and infected. We need a whole new outfit.

In the group session last week, we talked about putting on new behaviors and attitudes to replace the old sinful patterns. It is easy to see this process as though we are constructing our own garments of righteousness. We get a scrap of humility, a little patch of patience, a strip of love, and we try to sew them into garments for ourselves. These are the right materials, but we won't be able to come up with enough to cover ourselves. Real change, real righteousness, comes when we "put on Christ." By clothing ourselves with Christ, we exchange our old way of life for a relationship with Him. When we become Christ-followers, we become new people. Instead of focusing on fulfilling our desires, we turn our focus to Jesus. Instead of trying to construct our own garments of righteousness, we understand that only Jesus can provide what we need.

Read Galatians 3:26-27. Have you become a child of God "through faith in Christ" (verse 26)? What are some areas where you are trying to make your own garments? How can you "clothe" yourself with Christ instead?

_____

_____

_____

_____

_____

_____

_____

DEVOTIONALS

DAY 3

New Attitude

Do nothing out of selfish ambition or vain conceit, but in humility consider others better than yourselves. Each of you should look not only to your own interests, but also to the interests of others. Your attitude should be the same as that of Christ Jesus (Philippians 2:3-5).

The goal of every Christ-follower is to become more and more like Christ. In order to become like Christ, we have to know what He is like, and then try to imitate Him. One area where we all need Jesus' help and guidance is with the struggle of pride versus humility. Humans have a basic need to feel that they matter, that they are important in some way. It is true that we are important. We are so important to God that He sent His only Son to die on our behalf, to give us the opportunity to be made clean and to inherit eternal life. Knowing that God cares about us in this way should leave us free to forget ourselves. We don't need to prove our own importance—God has already proved that. Instead, He has given us an amazing example to follow. Jesus Christ was God, and yet He was willing to lay aside His high position and give His life for us. He taught us how to be humble and to say to others, "You matter to me more than my own comfort and position."

Read Philippians 2:6-11. What does this passage tell you about Christ's attitude? How can you imitate it and conquer the fatal distraction of pride?

_____

_____

_____

_____

_____

_____

_____

_____

_____

_____

_____

_____

DEVOTIONALS

DAY 4

How's Your Heart?

The LORD detests all the proud of heart. Be sure of this: They will not go unpunished (Proverbs 16:5).

Our defeated sinful human nature is still good at taking our natural desire to feel valued down the road to the sin of pride. In our culture, we talk a lot about self-image. Our problems are often blamed on a bad self-image. A good self-image is the "be-all" and "end-all" of life. Whatever we do, it has to make us feel good about ourselves. This sounds nice, but in actuality, "good self-image" is often just a nice euphemism for pride in ourselves. We spend so much time thinking about ourselves that we become proud, self-sufficient, and arrogant. We think that we are the center of the universe. God won't tolerate this kind of attitude. Scripture says that God detests pride in our hearts. He hates it, so much that a proud heart cannot be in His presence.

Read Matthew 5:3. How do those who are "poor in spirit" contrast with the "proud of heart"? On a scale of 1 (poor in spirit) to 10 (proud of heart), how would you rate your level of pride? What can you do to lower your score today?

_____

_____

_____

_____

_____

_____

_____

_____

_____

_____

_____

_____

_____

_____

DEVOTIONALS

DAY 5

Noses In The Air

When pride comes, then comes disgrace, but with humility comes wisdom (Proverbs 11:2).

The ironic thing about pride is that it accomplishes exactly the opposite of what we desire. Pride is often described as having its "nose in the air." Appropriately, this is also a good description of what happens to us when we are walking down the road of pride. When we have our nose in the air, we can't see where we're going, and sooner or later we will fall. Pride is exactly the same way. It has its gaze focused on self—it doesn't see the obstacles in the road, the scenery, or the needs of others. Eventually, pride is going to trip on something and fall flat.

In contrast, humility has its eyes open. It looks ahead at the obstacles on the road. It notices the needs of others. It is aware of what is happening, not just to itself, but also to everyone else. By having mind and heart open, humility gains wisdom, and with wisdom comes honor.

"A man's pride brings him low, but a man of lowly spirit gains honor" (Proverbs 29:23).

Write down one of these two proverbs on a card, and memorize it or tack it up somewhere where you will see it. Is your "nose up," or are your eyes open to the needs of others and the true state of your heart? How do you need to adjust your focus?

_____

_____

_____

_____

_____

_____

_____

_____

_____

_____

DEVOTIONALS

DAY 6

Are You Watching?

Now that I, your Lord and Teacher, have washed your feet, you also should wash one another's feet. I have set you an example that you should do as I have done for you. I tell you the truth, no servant is greater than his master, nor is a messenger greater than the one who sent him. Now that you know these things, you will be blessed if you do them (John 13:14-17).

Pride often makes us unable or unwilling to serve others. It can be as simple as feeling too important to do something for someone else. Other times pride keeps us so self-focused that we never even notice the needs of others.

In New Testament times, it was the custom to welcome guests by having a servant wash their feet. Jesus and His disciples didn't have a servant, and when they gathered to share the Passover meal, there was no one to wash feet. It didn't occur to one of them to humble himself and act as a servant to the others. Then Jesus, the most important person of all, the one they should have been falling all over themselves to serve, got up and did the job. He took the bowl of water and the towel, and He washed their feet.

"No servant is greater than his master." That means that not one of us is too important, too special, too beautiful, or too clever to do the lowest, dirtiest job for someone else. If Jesus, the only Son of God, and the Creator of the Universe, could be a servant, can we do less?

Read Matthew 20:25-28. One of the best ways to test yourself for pride (and to get rid of it!) is to get out and serve someone else—particularly someone toward whom you feel superior. Make a plan to serve someone else in the next 48 hours.

_____

_____

_____

_____

_____

_____

DEVOTIONALS

DAY 7

Motives Matter

Be careful not to do your "acts of righteousness" before men, to be seen by them. If you do, you will have no reward from your father in heaven. ... And when you pray, do not be like the hypocrites, for they love to pray standing in the synagogues and on the street corners to be seen by men. I tell you the truth, they have received their reward in full (Matthew 6:1,5).

Pride can be very sneaky. Did you know that we could be proud of our humility? We can also be proud of our own righteousness. Jesus gave some stern warnings about advertising our own humility and righteousness. We know that God wants us to have an attitude of humility and service toward others. He taught His disciples that those who want to be great in God's kingdom must be servants.

In our humanness, it is easy for us to take this as a simple appeal to pride. "Oh, good," we think, "Here is the godly way to be Number One. I can just do these little acts of service, and soon everyone will look up to me as a wonderful Christian example." Think again. If admiration is our goal in serving others, whatever praise we get is our reward in full (verse 5). God will not reward us. The only way to be great in God's kingdom is to glorify Him, and the only way to glorify God is through genuine humility. That means serving others "for real," with no ulterior motives.

Have you ever done something for someone else, and he or she didn't even say, "Thanks"? How did you feel? Looking back, what did that say about your motives? What are your motives today when you help others?

_____

_____

_____

_____

_____

_____

_____

_____

_____

_____

DEVOTIONALS

DAY 8

Not By Law

It was not through law that Abraham and his offspring received the promise that he would be heir of the world, but through the righteousness that comes by faith. For if those who live by law are heirs, faith has no value, and the promise is worthless, because law brings wrath (Romans 4:13-15a).

As we study what God's Word says about sin, it should convict us. We should want to change our lives to fit with God's pattern, in order to honor and please Him. But, because of our pride, some of us begin to believe that if we could just follow a set of rules, everything would be fine in the end. We think we have what it takes to make everything okay. This is an attitude of basic pride. Many of us struggle with this desire to be self-sufficient. We don't really want to be accountable to God for our actions, and we don't want to be indebted to one another. Pride never plays a role in true righteousness. We seek righteousness because we are a new creation, we are walking in the light, but we aren't comfortable in the old, filthy, infected garments anymore. We seek righteousness to glorify God. We seek righteousness because He has commanded us to seek it. But we can't make ourselves righteous.

We must never, never get the idea that changing our lives is going to make us acceptable to Him. Cleaning up our lives won't make us worthy of salvation. We can't earn our way into God's favor. If we could, then there was no need for Jesus to die. There would be no need for faith in God. Putting off the old and putting on the new only works if we have accepted God's free gift of salvation. This is something for which we can never ever pay. It is the gift of love.

Have you accepted this gift of salvation? Are you a part of God's family, or do you have the pride in your heart that thinks you can make it on your own? Read Colossians 2:20-23. Why do you think rules do not work for restraining sensual indulgence?

_____

_____

_____

_____

_____

_____

DEVOTIONALS

DAY 9

Free to Love

Therefore, there is now no condemnation for those who are in Christ Jesus, because through Christ Jesus the law of the Spirit of life set me free from the law of sin and death (Romans 8:1-2).

You, my brothers, were called to be free. But do not use your freedom to indulge the sinful nature; rather, serve one another in love (Galatians 5:13).

Following the rules cannot possibly save us because the law leads to punishment and death. Under the law, we are always condemned because we can never keep the law perfectly. We are always lawbreakers. Can you imagine what it would be like to constantly worry that the last rule you broke was the straw that broke the camel's back—that God might finally turn His back on you? But through Jesus, we are set free from this bondage to the law. We don't have to live in fear of rejection because we mess up the rules. Jesus already paid for our sins with His sacrificial death. But Jesus didn't die so that we could sin without fear of punishment. He died to set us free from the power of sin. Therefore, we should use our freedom to glorify God, not to satisfy our own desires.

Read Galatians 5:4-6. Make a list of some practical ways you could express your faith "through love" this week.

_____

_____

_____

_____

_____

_____

_____

_____

_____

_____

_____

_____

DEVOTIONALS

DAY 10

Down and Up

Humble yourselves, therefore, under God's mighty hand, that he may lift you up in due time. Cast all your anxiety on him because he cares for you (1 Peter 5:6-7).

In spite of our claims of self-sufficiency and arrogant attitudes, pride really stems from feelings of inadequacy and lack of trust in God. We fear that no one really cares about us, and believe that if we don't look out for ourselves, no one else will. When we sin, we are afraid to humble ourselves and ask for forgiveness. It takes security in knowing who God is, and who we are to God that gives us the ability to admit we are wrong, and that we are not the most important, the most beautiful, the most valuable, or the most of anything.

If we will risk our pride, our self-esteem, our perceived value, and humble ourselves before God, we will find that it is more than worth it. When God lifts us up He brings us to a place we could never reach by our own efforts. His care for us is more complete than anything we can do for ourselves. Get off the pride-ride today. It isn't worth the cost.

Where do you think your trust level is right now? In what areas of your life are you still entertaining pride?

_____

_____

_____

_____

_____

_____

_____

_____

_____

_____

_____

_____

_____

_____

Get Off the Pride Ride

Romans 12:3; Isaiah 14:12-15; Psalm 138:6;
Deuteronomy 8:17-19; 1 Peter 5:5-7

Drive by an airport sometime and watch all the planes taking off. You will be observing thousands of people of all ages taking trips. Some are taking business trips. Some are taking trips for pleasure. In this session on fatal distractions, we will look at a very popular trip, a trip that every one of us has taken—the ego trip. This trip is fueled by pride, and our destination is a universe called "me."

Notice that the word "pride" is the word "ride" with the letter "P" in front. This describes an ego trip well, as it is essentially a P-ride or a pride ride. Pride can be defined as an inordinate amount of self-esteem, or more accurately, looking out for "number one"—yourself and your own interests. Its synonyms aren't that attractive: arrogance, egotism, vanity, vainglory. Most of us, when we think about pride, picture a big-mouthed, ostentatious, outlandish type of person. However, this is not necessarily a true picture. Some of the proudest people can appear meek, mild, and conservative.

START IT UP

We have observed people around us taking ego trips at any place and time. From these observations we all have in our minds some images of a really proud or arrogant person, someone who is practically the definition of pride.

1. What fictional character (from a movie, TV show, or book) do you think of as a classic example of pride?

2.   What characteristics does this fictional character have that really demonstrate this trait of pride?

TALK IT UP

Pride is a frightening thing. It blinds itself to its own presence. It leaps up everywhere in our lives. It comes early and stays late. It has a cup of coffee with us in the morning, and it puts us to bed at night. Pride is first in our study on fatal distractions and on the list of the Seven Deadly Sins, because it is the forerunner of all sins. Pride makes us feel self-sufficient, invincible, and all-knowing. This puts us in the most vulnerable position possible for succumbing to the temptations of this world.

Self-Concept or Self-Conceit?

Self-esteem is a popular issue in our day and age. We think that poor self-esteem has to be remedied by learning to feel good about ourselves. In actuality, poor self-esteem is a subtle form of self-centeredness. Those people with a poor self-concept may not realize it, but pride is taking them for a ride. Pride focuses on "me, me, me," whether it is "poor little me, me, me," or "look at wonderful me, me, me." Instead of working so hard to enhance our self-concept, we should be looking for a stronger "God-concept."

By now, some of you are probably thinking, "Wait. I thought it was important to have good self-esteem. That is what I learned in school. Everyone has to have a good self-concept. We are supposed to take pride in ourselves." This is true, if the reasons for good self-esteem are based on God's truth in the Bible. When we have "good self-esteem" because we see ourselves the way God sees us (with unconditional love), then that is great. If we feel confident because we know that Christ died for us so we are forgiven and bound for heaven, then that is right. The problem is that in today's culture we are taught to feel good about ourselves no matter what, which can cover a multitude of sins and rebellion. When we sin, we are supposed to feel bad because sin separates us from God and damages all of our relationships. The bottom line is that a good self-concept has to come from understanding and accepting that God loves you no matter what.

Read Romans 12:3

3. How can we tell the difference between a proper self-concept and self-conceit?

Read Isaiah 14:12-15

To understand more about pride, we need to go way back before Adam and Eve and take a look at Lucifer (otherwise known as Satan). Satan was originally an incredible angel; the most important of God's created beings. He had a high place in heaven and everything should have been great. But instead, he listened to pride. He wanted to be the biggest and best, to the point of wanting to take over God's place. Read these verses again. Notice how many times Lucifer says, "I will, I will, I will." He became so self-centered that he thought he was more than God. Because of his rebellion, God cast him from His presence. But Satan wasn't satisfied. He passed the infection of pride on to our "parents," Adam and Eve. Once they climbed aboard the ego trip, the pattern began and we human beings have been struggling with our focus on "self" ever since.

4. How do we, as humans, try to put ourselves in God's place?

The Poison of Pride: Damaging Our Relationship with God

When we first begin to welcome pride into our lives, it doesn't look that bad. Pride makes us feel good, and we don't see where it will lead us. It damages our relationship with God little by little.

Read Psalm 138:6

One of the first results of being proud is that it distances us from God. Pride is sneaky. We don't even realize that we are slowly moving away from God. So, how can we find out if we are taking the pride ride? It's really easy. Take the following test.

(1) How much interest do you have in worshiping God? If you lack interest in

worshiping God, you are probably on a pride ride. Prideful people see everything orbiting around themselves. "My schedule, my time, my dating life, my vacation plan, my activities …" They worship themselves. As a result, God takes a backseat and He doesn't receive much of their worship.

(2) What are you including in your prayers? To find out, write out your prayers for a few days. Then go back and look at them a few weeks later. What do you see? Are you prayers "me-centered"? Or do you spend prayer time worshiping God?

(3) How involved are you in ministry at your church? A symptom of taking the pride ride is a lack of involvement. You see, ministry requires humility. We can't serve people when we feel that we are above them. So often, we are just like the disciples at the Last Supper. They didn't have a servant to wash their feet, and not one of them was about to get up and do it for everyone else. They just ignored their dirty feet and let it go. But not Jesus, He gave His disciples an example of humble service and got up and washed all their feet for them. (See John 13:1-17.) There is no room for pride in service.

5. What impresses you most about Jesus washing the disciples' feet?

Read Deuteronomy 8:17-19

Lack of appreciation for God's workmanship is a glaring sign that we are harboring pride. Often when we do something special, like get a promotion, get a great creative idea, or give a really effective speech, we feel that we have done it all. We think, "I did that! I am so tenacious. I am so disciplined. I am such a leader. I have such a winsome personality. I am just something else!" We fail to give the credit to God, not just in our words, but also in how we actually live our life.

6. What will look different in our lives if we are giving God the credit for our accomplishments?

The Poison of Pride: Damaging Our Relationship with People

The ride of pride not only distances us from God, it distances us from others. How can we tell if we are distancing ourselves from others? Take the following test.

(1) How do you respond when someone hurts you? Do you begin the reconciliation process, or do you refuse to forgive until the other person comes and apologizes? Pride can keep us from being openhearted and forgiving, but Jesus shows us another way. The Bible says that while we were still sinners, Christ died for us. He made the first move. He didn't wait until it looked like we were sorry for our sins. He came to us, and He took the initiative. Reconciliation is the one place where we are all supposed to be saying, "Me first! Let me be first to reconcile."

When we refuse to reconcile, the results can be devastating. Marriages are destroyed, relationships are fragmented, and businesses are lost. Pride can so dominate us that we white-knuckle the throttle on our ego trip and refuse to make the first move toward reconciliation.

(2) Do you manipulate others to make yourself look good? We know that pride has started distancing us from others if we are manipulating people in our lives. For example, some parents really want to elevate themselves by having amazing children. Their simple, unselfish appreciation for their children and desire to see them succeed turns into an unhealthy version of pride. They push their children to succeed so that they look good. An unselfish and proper "pride" in others includes wanting the best for them and rejoicing in their success for their sake, not our own.

(3) Do you find that you are talking about yourself a lot, rather than being interested in what others are doing? The most obvious way that pride distances us from others is through self-centered conversation. We all know someone who can't stop talking about himself or herself. No one enjoys talking to people who are only interested in their own ideas or experiences. Instead of reaching out and drawing other people closer, this kind of conversation points in and repels people.

7. Think about your primary relationships. What are some ways that pride has caused distance in these relationships?

The Pride Ride, Illustrated

To make this "pride ride" picture really stick, lets just take a look at the first-class section of our flight. Here is the passenger list:

Velma Vanity: She constantly has a mirror in front of her face. She is always thinking about her appearance. She looks down on people who don't look "put together" enough.

Eddie Education: He is always dropping degrees. "Yes, I graduated from an Ivy League School. I have my MBA, PhD, WXYZ."

Anna Accomplishment: She has awards and trophies and ribbons all over her. She doesn't mind telling you how she won each one.

Ronnie Reverse: This guy looks out of place in first class. He is a reverse snob. He dresses down, and he looks down his nose at the upper class. He takes pride in looking lower class, in keeping up the opposite image of the "rich snobs."

Ned Namedropper: He is always talking about the important people he knows. He makes it sound like professional athletes, celebrities, Hollywood stars, and power brokers are his best friends.

Martha Materialism: Everything she owns has a name brand. Her house, her car, and her swimming pool are all the latest models. Her deepest interests are the size of her bank account and the latest new thing to own.

Get Off the Pride Ride

How happy and content do you think these people in first class are? The result of pride is <u>always </u>discontentment. The proudest people are those who are not really relaxed and at peace with themselves. So here is what we have to do on the pride ride. We have to throttle back, put the seats and tray tables in upright and locked position. We have to land, taxi, and get off the plane. And then we have to strip off our garments of pride.

Read 1 Peter 5:5-7

In our last session we talked about the importance of replacing our old clothes with God's new designer garment. This new garment replaces the rags of pride with humility. Peter calls us to "clothe yourselves with humility" (verse 5). This does not mean demeaning ourselves—this is false humility and is still "me-centered." True humility is actually thinking of others first. Really humble people become so

"others-centered" that they stop worrying about themselves completely.

How do we clothe ourselves with humility? *First, we need to spend time daily worshiping God.* When we see ourselves before God, we are humbled by His holiness and love. There isn't any room for self-conceit when we are standing before God and looking into His face. We can't remain proud and elitist when we are spending time with the Man who chose prostitutes, tax collectors, and sinners for His friends. We can't stand before the cross and still be proud.

8. What are some practical ways we can spend time daily worshipping God?

Second, we need to thank God and appreciate His workmanship. Yes, you can take a compliment and say, "Thank you very much," but remember Who gave you that talent or ability. Remember who blessed you.

Third, we need to get immersed in ministry. When we choose to "wash the feet" of others, we are putting action behind our humility.

9. In what ways does God "oppose the proud" (verse 5)? Have you felt this opposition in your life?

LIFT IT UP

The saddest consequence of the ride of pride is that it can keep us from eternity with the Lord Himself. Pride is keeping scores of people from Christianity. It tells people that if they live a better-than-average life on planet earth, God will give them heaven. Pride also tells people that if they are really strong and sincere in what they believe, then they will deserve heaven. However, the Bible says that we are saved by grace (which is undeserved favor), through faith, and not by works so that no one can boast (see Ephesians 2:8-9). There is nothing that any one of us could do or say to be good enough to deserve salvation. We have to admit our pride, turn from it, and ask Jesus to come into our hearts and lives.

10. Is pride keeping you from heaven? If it is not keeping you from heaven, is it keeping you from a deeper relationship with God and with others? How can this group pray for you?

11. What is one thing you can do in the coming week to clothe yourself with humility?

Take time to pray specifically for each other in those areas where you need to replace pride with humility.

My Prayer Needs:

_____

_____

My Group's Prayer Needs: _____

_____

_____

_____

_____

_____

_____

_____

_____

_____

DEVOTIONALS

DAY 1

Who Wants to Be a Fool?

The end of a matter is better than its beginning, and patience is better than pride. Do not be quickly provoked in your spirit, for anger resides in the lap of fools (Ecclesiastes 7:8-9).

In a way, all of the fatal distractions (or Seven Deadly Sins) are related to one another. A particular sin never comes alone. It brings its relatives, and settles down. If you let it stay, it invites its cousins and in-laws, along with their friends as well. Pride does just that. If you harbor pride, it will invite its closest relative, anger, in to stay with you. Pride leads to anger for a simple reason—when we are on the pride-ride, we think that we are the most important person around. Therefore, if anyone offends us, even accidentally, we feel like that person is attacking our very being. They have wounded the ego and trampled on the self-image of Number One, and that is unforgivable. But that's not the way God looks at it. He says that you'll make a fool of yourself if you are easily angered. Anger is a powerful emotion—it is hot, and it can be damaging. If we jump in without looking, we are going to end up causing all kinds of unnecessary damage.

Are you easily angered? When you are angry, do you feel that you have the right to be "mad"? Because anger is the great justifier, it can be hard to identify an anger problem in your life. Keep track of yourself for a week. Make a mark on your calendar for every time you feel yourself getting hot under the collar. You might be surprised at how often you indulge.

_____

_____

_____

_____

_____

_____

_____

_____

_____

_____

DAY 2

Leaving Footholds

"In your anger, do not sin": Do not let the sun go down while you are still angry, and do not give the devil a foothold (Ephesians 4:26-27).

As we are discussing the subject of anger, it is important to realize that anger is not necessarily a sin. God didn't say, "Never feel angry." He said, "Don't let it lead you into sin." The emotion of anger is one that will crop up in our lives over and over again. The key to staying out of sin is in how we handle the anger. This passage gives us the first important tool for handling anger: Take care of it on the same day. Don't ever let anger fester. When you let anger fester, when you hold onto it, feed it, and think about it, it will develop into resentment and bitterness. If you keep your anger overnight, you are giving Satan a foothold in your life. It is just as if you pounded a few stakes into the cliff to make it easier for him to climb into your life.

With whom do you tend to fight or feel angry at most often? Have you dealt with this, either with God or with that person? Don't let the sun go down on your anger tonight.

_____

_____

_____

_____

_____

_____

_____

_____

_____

_____

_____

_____

_____

DAY 3

Righteous Anger

So Israel joined in worshiping the Baal of Peor. And the LORD's anger burned against them (Numbers 25:3).

It may come as a surprise, but most of the references to anger in the Bible are talking about God's anger. Remember, anger doesn't necessarily lead to sin. It is a real emotion, and there are times when anger is an appropriate feeling. When God saw His chosen people, the people He had miraculously saved from Egypt and had fed in the wilderness for 40 years, turn to worshipping other gods, He was angry. When the Israelites sacrificed their children to idols, God was angry. He didn't just say, "Love and peace, acceptance and harmony." He punished them. When we see the innocent suffering, when we see people harming others on purpose, it is not wrong to feel angry. We are experiencing righteous anger. These things make God angry, too. However, we still have to remember the key: do not sin in your anger. God is completely holy and He can handle anger without sinning. We aren't and we can't. Even our righteous anger is something that we have to turn over to God, asking Him to help us deal with it and direct it in a way that will honor Him and help others.

Righteous anger can be a powerful force for changing bad patterns and sinful behaviors. Is there something that makes you feel righteous anger right now? Spend time praying about how you should react.

_____

_____

_____

_____

_____

_____

_____

_____

_____

_____

DAY 4

Attack of the Killer Tongue

All kinds of animals, birds, reptiles and creatures of the sea are being tamed and have been tamed by man, but no man can tame the tongue. It is a restless evil, full of deadly poison. With the tongue we praise our Lord and Father, and with it we curse men, who have been made in God's likeness. Out of the same mouth come praise and cursing. My brothers, this should not be (James 3:7-10).

For sinful, weak humans, handling anger can be like handling a fire hose turned on full blast. If we can direct the force in the right direction, anger can be a tool. But too often it twists out of our grasp and blasts something to pieces. The power is too much for us.

One of the first places this happens is in the area of the tongue. When we get mad, almost the first thing we do is open our mouths. We say whatever comes to the top first, and it usually isn't pretty. It is amazing what terrible things we have right at the tips of our tongues. Every one of us can look back and think of some hurtful thing we said, probably to someone we love, that we didn't even really believe. Anger is a great fuel for the evil side of the tongue.

Have you had a recent "attack of the killer tongue" for which you need to apologize? Eating a lot of humble pie is usually a good tongue tamer. What would help you avoid these attacks in the future?

_____

_____

_____

_____

_____

_____

_____

_____

_____

_____

DEVOTIONALS

DAY 5

Rhythm of Life

My dear brothers, take note of this. Everyone should be quick to listen, slow to speak and slow to become angry, for man's anger does not bring about the righteous life that God desires (James 1:19-20).

Most of us are quick to become angry, even quicker to start talking, but very slow to listen. We have the pattern backward. Emotion comes first; reaction follows right on top of it, and rational thought is a slow third. This is the natural, easy way to handle problems. But it doesn't work. Emotions are volatile and are set off by anything and nothing. They don't necessarily correspond with reality. When we act on emotion, we are just as likely as not to be wrong. Instead, God has given us a different pattern. It isn't as easy, and it takes work. But it has the best results. His pattern goes like this: Gather information so you can think rationally (be quick to listen). After you've thought it through carefully, act on it (be slow to speak). Then let the emotions follow the thought and action (be slow to become angry).

Did you catch James' rhythm? Quick, slow, slow. What is the rhythm in your life? What order do you usually react in? What do you need to change to get more in step with God's rhythm?

_____

_____

_____

_____

_____

_____

_____

_____

_____

_____

_____

_____

_____

DEVOTIONALS

DAY 6

Tearing Down, Building Up

Do not let any unwholesome talk come out of your mouths, but only what is helpful for building others up according to their needs, that it may benefit those who listen. And do not grieve the Holy Spirit of God, with whom you were sealed for the day of redemption. Get rid of all bitterness, rage and anger, brawling and slander, along with every form of malice. Be kind and compassionate to one another, forgiving each other, just as in Christ God forgave you (Ephesians 4:29-32).

Reacting to our anger and shooting off at the mouth is something that many of us don't take very seriously. We excuse ourselves by saying, "Well, I just got mad. I didn't really mean what I said." We need to realize that when wrong things come out of our mouths, we grieve the Holy Spirit. What we say when we are mad really does matter to God. Instead of responding in anger to one another, we have to learn to be forgiving. God has freely forgiven each one of us, because of Christ's death on the cross. In the same way, He expects us to extend forgiveness, kindness, and compassion toward one another. God's Word sometimes uses a great phrase for this concept. It is "loving kindness." That says it all. When we are showing loving kindness to one another, there won't be room for anger and bitter words.

What are some things that you could do to build up the other people in your life, rather than tear them down?

DAY 7

Who's the Strongest?

A man's wisdom gives him patience; it is to his glory to overlook an offense (Proverbs 19:11).

Many times, we feel that ignoring an offense is a slight on our character. We feel like the gunslingers in the old westerns. If we don't fight an insult, we'll be branded as cowards, and no one will respect us again. Essentially, if we don't fight back, we feel that we are agreeing with the person who offended us. It takes a lot more wisdom than most of us have to look past the initial sting of the insult, and see the future results. Which is harder, flying into a rage when someone offends you, or keeping your cool? Which requires greater strength? Which shows the most discipline?

It is tempting to pay back insult for insult, injury for injury. Patience is definitely not the easy road, but it pays off in the end. When we respond in anger to an offense, we usually over-react. We not only pay back, we punish. The other person then feels just as offended and retaliates back. The cycle only stops when one person has the strength, the wisdom, and the love to patiently look past an offense.

A patient man has great understanding, but a quick tempered man displays folly (Proverbs 14:29).

When has someone hurt your feelings or really annoyed you recently? How did you respond? How could you respond better in the future?

_____

_____

_____

_____

_____

_____

_____

_____

_____

DEVOTIONALS

DAY 8

It's the Attitude

You have heard that it was said to the people long ago, "Do not murder, and anyone who murders will be subject to judgment." But I tell you that anyone who is angry with his brother will be subject to judgment (Matthew 5:21-22a).

"Sticks and stones may break my bones, but words can never hurt me." Most of us know that this saying isn't really true. Hard words do hurt us, even though the bruises don't show. But we still act as if we believe it when it comes to the way we ourselves act. We don't throw sticks and stones, but we don't mind throwing angry words. In addition, we don't really believe that it matters. We are so used to our anger that we don't see the sin.

The Law of the Old Testament said that murder is sin. However, Jesus takes us a big step further. Jesus is always interested in what is in our hearts, not just in what we do with our actions. Yes, murder is sin. But did you realize that harboring anger toward your brother is also sin that will lead to judgment? What we do comes out of what is in our hearts, and if what is in our hearts is evil, the outside will eventually match the inside.

Read Matthew 23:25-26. Only Jesus can clean the inside of your "cup and dish." Have you asked Him to do this, or are you still trying to polish your heart on your own? What anger do you especially need cleaned out today?

_____

_____

_____

_____

_____

_____

_____

_____

_____

_____

DAY 9

The Escalator

As the LORD looked with favor on Abel and his offering, but on Cain and his offering he did not look with favor. So Cain was very angry, and his face was downcast (Genesis 4:4b-5).

Anyone who hates his brother is a murderer, and you know that no murderer has eternal life in him (1 John 3:15).

Anger is first mentioned in the Bible in the story of Cain and Abel. Cain was angry because God accepted his brother's offering, but not his. Cain harbored his anger and it grew, as anger does. It turned into hatred, and one day Cain murdered his brother.

Any one of us would recoil from the idea of murdering someone. Everyone agrees on that sin, whether or not they follow Christ. Murdering is against God's law, and it is against civil law. If you murder someone, you will be behind bars. No one will tolerate it. Yet we tolerate the drive behind murder all the time. We harbor anger, we foster hatred, and we still think that we are all right. We forget that God looks right into our hearts. That attitude of hatred is an attitude of murder, and in God's book, attitude is sin just as much as action.

How can you keep the emotion of anger from turning into the sin of hatred? What if someone has really hurt you?

_____

_____

_____

_____

_____

_____

_____

_____

_____

_____

DAY 10

The High Road

You have heard that it was said, "Love your neighbor and hate your enemy." But I tell you: Love your enemies and pray for those who persecute you …. If you love those who love you, what reward will you get? Are not even the tax collectors doing that? And if you greet only your brothers, what are you doing more than others? Do not even pagans do that? (Matthew 5:43-44,46-47).

It's pretty clear we are to love other Christ-followers. After all, God has forgiven their sins just as much as He has ours. Someday we will be together in heaven. All this makes sense. But then Jesus takes us a step further. We are also commanded to love our enemies. Not even the "bad guys" are fair game for our hatred.

God has called us to a higher level of discipleship. We don't get the easy road, of loving just the nice people or the people who care about us. We are required to show love to those who are against us. God didn't give us this command just because He felt sorry for our enemies. It wasn't just to make life a little harder for us. When we harbor anger, even justifiable anger, it will turn to bitterness and resentment. It will spoil inside us, and we will become sour, bitter, and unlovely. Keeping anger going requires dwelling on the sins of our enemies, and dwelling on sin will twist us. We have to hand our anger back to God.

Whom do you have the hardest time loving right now? Acknowledge to yourself what this person did that angered you, and then specifically forgive each offense before God. Even if you are not able to reconcile with the person, if you have taken care of your end of the forgiveness and repentance, you will be able to move on in your walk with the Lord.

_____

_____

_____

_____

_____

_____

_____

Unravel Anger...
Before It Unravels You

Ephesians 4:26; Genesis 37:3-20; Genesis 4:1-12; Proverbs 12:18; James 3:6; Ephesians 4:31-32

"I'm furious. That really annoys me. I'm so mad I could …" These expressions describe an emotion that is central, far-reaching, and complex. This emotion is known as anger, and it is the next topic in our study on fatal distractions. Anger is everywhere. It is a guest in our homes. It is with us in marriage and child rearing. It rides in our cars. It sits beside us at work. It plays in our foursomes. It stands behind us while we are waiting in the grocery store express checkout lane. We are never going to get away from it so we have to learn how to deal with it in a godly manner; not just outwardly but in our hearts as well.

START IT UP

All of us have experienced both being angry and making others angry. Often we regret those things we do and say in a moment of anger.

1. What memories do you have about anger in your family when you were growing up?

2. Describe a time when a friend or family member made you really mad. What did you do?

TALK IT UP

The Bible uses two words to describe anger. They mean, "to grow hot" and "flared nostrils." Isn't that classic? When someone gets angry, they do get hot and their nostrils flare. Anger can also be an enjoyable sin. It is one of the most common of the fatal distractions, because it feels good to get angry, to lick our wounds, and to think how we will get back at someone for hurting us. We love to just "let it all out"! Many social commentators describe this era as the "Age of Rage." We live in a world with drive-by shootings, battered women, and pipe bombs. It would be easy to think that we should just move off to a desert island somewhere and escape all this anger. Yet the Bible says that we should influence others for the kingdom of God within the Age of Rage.

How We Handle Anger

Anger is a physical emotion. When we get angry, our adrenalin starts pumping, our blood pressure increases, our mouths get dry, our palms get sweaty, and our muscles tense. We are ready to go. This emotion is intense, it is physical, and we have to learn how to handle it in a positive way. But first, let's look at some of the negative ways that people use to handle anger.

Some people deal with anger like toxic waste. Toxic waste is buried, and we are assured that everything is okay. Then years later it begins to leak underground, shows up in the water system, and causes people to get sick. When we bury anger and think that it is over and done with, no problem, it begins to leak internally. This leak can cause our attitudes, relationships, and ultimately our faith to become sick and weak.

Others deal with anger like a volcano. They rumble and rumble. They say to themselves, "I've been taking this for too long. Today I am going to tell this person off." They spew hot lava and volcanic ash over the entire situation, and the only thing left is charred remains. Volcanic people never try to reconcile relationships and never apologize for being angry.

Still others deal with anger like they are a snow cone. Someone makes them upset and they give them the cold shoulder. "Oh, nothing is wrong. I'm fine. It's okay." Yet they are angry on the inside, icing people out.

Then there are the microwave people. They are talking along, no big deal, and then

one little thing hits them wrong and they press, "TIME, COOK, 5 Seconds." Boom. It's over, and the other person is cooked.

Did you see yourself in any of the above examples? If we can understand ourselves and how we handle anger, maybe it will help us to overcome this fatal distraction. Perhaps this is why the Apostle Paul told young Timothy to "Watch your life and doctrine closely" (1 Timothy 4:16). In other words, "Study your thoughts. Unravel your complex emotions in the light of God's truth."

3. Which of these examples above most closely describes how you deal with your anger?

4. Is it selfish or inconsiderate to require others to help you work through your emotions? Why or why not?

Unraveling Anger

Let's take the Apostle Paul's advice and attempt to unravel this complex emotion.

Read Ephesians 4:26

This verse points us to a very important concept. In and of itself, anger is not necessarily a sin. Anger by itself is neutral, similar to a crowbar. A crowbar can be used for good—if a window is stuck or if a door is jammed. But a crowbar can also be used to bash someone in the head or to break into someone's home. Anger is the same. It can be used positively or negatively.

Constructive anger helps us to change things that need to be changed. For instance, if we fail to do what is right and end up losing something we really wanted because of our own fault, we might be angry. If we take that anger and blame others or turn it inward and become depressed, then our anger becomes destructive. But if we channel that anger and strong emotional energy to help us change the way we live, then it becomes constructive.

42

Sometimes as Christians we think we should never get angry. We feel we need to show love, joy, peace, forgiveness, and "Kum Ba Yah," 24 hours a day, seven days a week. It is true—those are the traits of a Christ-follower. But it is also true there is such a thing as righteous anger. God gets angry, and He gets angry at one thing—sin. When we get angry because of sin we are experiencing righteous anger. It is right to be angry when we see parents abusing their children. It is right to be angry when we see people mistreated because of their skin color or socioeconomic class. These things make God angry, too.

5. What examples of constructive anger have you seen in others? How can you apply this to your life?

Analogies of Anger

Now that we've got all that straight, look again at verse 26 in Ephesians 4 for a really important piece of advice—don't sleep on your anger. We often think that anger will evaporate overnight, but it doesn't. It's like a *poison* that will concentrate and gradually destroy us from the inside out. When we go to bed angry, day after day, week after week, the problems are never solved. They just keep growing into bigger and bigger problems.

6. Does not going to bed angry mean that it is wrong to stop and cool off before confronting a problem? How can we tell when something needs to be thrashed through and when it should be laid to rest for a brief time?

Read Genesis 37:3-20

Anger is also like a *trapeze*. You see, anger is not the first emotion most of us feel in a situation. It is often the second emotion. Think about what happened to Joseph's brothers. When they saw that their father was playing favorites, they

were first hurt and jealous. Instead of dealing with these emotions of hurt and jealousy, they grabbed hold of the trapeze of anger and swung right over their first emotions into hatred and murderous intent. Hate is a lot stronger than jealousy or hurt, but anger carried them far beyond the first emotion. It was a lot easier to be angry than to deal with their emotions in a constructive way.

7. Can you think of a time when anger carried you past your first emotion of hurt or worry and made you do something mean? In retrospect, how do you think you could have handled this without swinging on the trapeze of anger?

Read Genesis 4:1-12

We have seen how anger can be like a trapeze and a poison. Anger is also like a *door* that leads to other sins. When God accepted Abel's sacrifice and rejected Cain's, Cain was angry. God knew that he was angry and He warned Cain of the dangers of anger. Cain had a choice. He could have admitted the feelings of anger that he was experiencing, confessed them to God, and been made right. Instead, Cain opened the door of anger, and it led straight to murder.

Anger runs with a really nasty friend named "Revenge." If we entertain our feelings of anger and open that door, revenge is one of the first friends that gets invited in. We waste so much time and energy trying to get back at people who have hurt us. When we take revenge into our own hands, we are elbowing God out of the way. Romans 12:19 tells us that dealing with sin in others is always God's job. He can do a much better job of it than we could ever dream of doing. We just end up creating more damage.

8. Probably most of us are too "civilized" to murder our family members, but that isn't the only sin to which anger leads. What other sins crouch outside the anger door?

Read Proverbs 12:18 and James 3:6

Angry or "reckless" words can pierce like a *sword*. Have you ever said some things when you were angry that you wish you could take back? The tongue is almost always the first place we slip up when we are angry. It is easy to say, "Oh, I didn't really mean it. You should know I only said that because I was mad." Nevertheless, those cruel words do hurt the person you lashed out at. Angry words are also like a *fire*. They start with only a small spark, but before long the fire is out of control. Relationships can be burned to cinders, reputations destroyed, and people injured all because of a few little words.

Short-Circuiting Anger

So, what do we do about this fatal distraction? We can't get away from feelings of anger, so where do we go from here?

Read Ephesians 4:31-32

The answer is simple—just get rid of anger and all its friends. Isn't that one of the most frustrating pieces of advice there is? Just get rid of it. It doesn't seem that easy, does it? But don't give up yet. Verse 32 gives us the key. God doesn't just say, "Get rid of anger," He tells us to put on something else—kindness, compassion, and forgiveness. As we talked about in Session 1: when we give our lives to Jesus Christ, He gives us new clothing to wear. We no longer have to wear threads like anger, bitterness, revenge, and rage. Instead, we have a stunning outfit custom-designed just for us. When we choose to put it on, we look just like Christ.

Here are some quick practical ways to take off anger and put on kindness and forgiveness. Think about the person in your life who most often angers you. It's probably someone with whom you live or work. Next, imagine how you could help the relationship by trying the following behavior changes.

a) *Affirm the relationship.* Make sure that you let him know that he really matters to you.

b) *Negotiate with "I feel" statements.* Don't bring out the machine gun and riddle him with "You never" or "You always" statements.

c) *Guard the volume level.* Proverbs 15:1 tells us, "A gentle answer turns away wrath, but a harsh word stirs up anger."

d) *Establish resolve.* Have the attitude of always wanting to make the relationship better. If the other person does not want to deal with you, and you have sincerely tried to mend the relationship, then there may be nothing else you can do. But you have to try, even to the point of inviting your pastor or a trained mediator to assist you.

e) *Release the person.* Often when we've been hurt by someone, we feel that we can't let go of the conflict. We keep trying to go back and justify our position or make the other person see where she was wrong. At some point, we have to let go and extend forgiveness. But we can't always do it in one movement. We must continually ask God to help us release the person from the clutches of our anger, and hand the problem over to God. Remember, it's His job to deal with the other person, not ours.

LIFT IT UP

Psychologists teach that it is wrong to suppress anger, because anger turned inward will make us crazy. The Bible teaches that it is wrong to act out our anger, because it damages us and it damages others. So how do we resolve this dilemma? The key is in how we express our anger. When we start to see red, we can't just tie the lid on with bungee cords and repeat, "I'm not mad, I'm not angry, I'm not upset, everything is okay" 11 times and then be done with it. But we can't just let it spew all over the place and burn everyone around us, either. We have to be able to say to ourselves and to God, "Yes, I am very angry. This is what made me angry. I don't want to damage others, but I will, in a spirit of love, acknowledge how I feel. God, help me to keep calm and leave the revenge up to You. Help me to keep the anger door shut, showing kindness, mercy, and forgiveness, instead of reacting to what I feel." When we can do this, when we can label our anger and then leave it with God, we will be able to handle it and use it constructively. We will be able to be angry without sinning and to follow in Christ's footsteps.

9. In what situations do you struggle with feelings of anger? How can this group pray for you as you seek to handle this in a God-honoring manner?

10. Is there someone who has hurt you that you need to release right now? What steps do you need to take to initiate reconciliation?

Take time to pray specifically for each other in those areas where you are having a difficult time dealing with anger and resentment. Pray for those who have hurt you in the past.

My Prayer Needs:

_____

_____

_____

_____

_____

_____

_____

My Group's Prayer Needs:

_____

_____

_____

_____

_____

_____

_____

_____

_____

_____

DEVOTIONALS

DAY 1

The Blast of Envy

Anger is cruel and fury overwhelming, but who can stand before jealousy? (Proverbs 27:4).

Anger. Fury. Jealousy. Envy. These are ugly words, which bring up pictures of ugly things. When we are in the grip of anger, we hurt others. Envy is inward, but it can result in the same kind of destructive lashing out. Anger and envy often occur together. We want what others have and become angry when we can't have it. We somehow blame others for our discontent and lack of what we think we need. A person who has a problem with envy will cause destruction wherever he or she goes. Anger is a hot emotion that is often short lived. However, envy is something that has to be cultivated. It settles in and takes over a life, and then that life becomes a destructive force.

Envy is often unidentified in our lives. Of whom or what have you felt envious? Is this envy still being cultivated in your life, or have you dealt with it?

_____

_____

_____

_____

_____

_____

_____

_____

_____

_____

_____

_____

_____

_____

_____

_____

_____

_____

DAY 2

Thoughts That Rot

A heart at peace gives life to the body, but envy rots the bones (Proverbs 14:30).

It is true that envy and jealousy will often make us lash out and hurt those we envy. But envy is also destructive to the person who harbors it. Even if you never express your envy through your words or actions, if you have envy in your heart it will hurt you. Envy will make you discontented, insecure, and unhappy. An envious heart is never at peace, and a heart never at peace makes for an uncomfortable life.

Envy tears us down, rather than building us up. It wants to make everyone else just as miserable or poor or sinful as it is. It breeds bitterness, selfishness, and sin. It will "rot" our character and make us slowly go bad inside. Have you ever smelled something really rotten? The stench can be overpowering. That is what God says envy will do to us if we keep it around. It's like dropping a stink bomb into our lives.

Is your heart at peace, or do you smell your "bones rotting"? What do you think might be contributing to the lack of peace in your heart? (You may not have identified envy as the culprit, but try that thought on and see if it fits.)

_____

_____

_____

_____

_____

_____

_____

_____

_____

_____

_____

_____

_____

DEVOTIONALS

DAY 3

Keeping in Step

Since we live by the Spirit, let us keep in step with the Spirit. Let us not become conceited, provoking and envying each other (Galatians 5:25-26).

Envy is a sin related to both pride and anger. It is usually rooted in the conceited "me-first" attitude of pride. We are so busy thinking about Number One, that we think any good thing should be ours by right. We think everyone else should put us first, too! Frustrated envy then often leads to anger. We are jealous of others' accomplishments, possessions, or blessings; instead of being glad that they are happy, we want to take it away. We begin to resent those who have what we want, and resentment leads to picking fights with them or trying to bring them down to our level.

When we belong to Christ, we are marching hand-in-hand with the Holy Spirit. Our old pattern of conceit, envy, and quarreling is out of step. When we march this way, we are constantly pulling in the wrong direction. We can't be at peace. Instead, we need to stop and listen to the Holy Spirit's rhythm. We need to learn to march to a different tune, as we follow our leader—Jesus Christ.

Are you in step with the Holy Spirit – which leads to peace – or are you offbeat? What needs to change to get you in step with God?

_____

_____

_____

_____

_____

_____

_____

_____

_____

_____

_____

_____

DEVOTIONALS

DAY 4

I Hate You, You Hate Me

At one time we too were foolish, disobedient, deceived and enslaved by all kinds of passions and pleasures. We lived in malice and envy, being hated and hating one another. But when the kindness and love of God our Savior appeared, he saved us, not because of righteous things we had done, but because of his mercy. He saved us through the washing of rebirth and renewal by the Holy Spirit (Titus 3:3-5).

Although we all need to be loved and matter to others, the old patterns of envy don't make us very lovable. An envious person isn't very nice to be around. Envy produces negative conversation and words that tear down others. When we entertain envy, we look at others and hate what we see. When we are full of envy, we will soon be isolated on our own little islands of self. Envy separates people.

Envy is plain ugly. God hates it. Nevertheless, He didn't wait until we had cleaned up the envy in our lives to reach out to us. He didn't say, "Learn to love one another, and then come to me." He demonstrated the opposite of envy—in kindness and love, He came and saved us. We didn't do anything to deserve it. We couldn't have. Hatred and envy, physical passions and pleasures still entangled us.

So how do we free ourselves from envy? We must experience the "washing of rebirth and renewal by the Holy Spirit" (verse 5). When we have eternity in perspective, the little things of this world will not seem so important anymore.

Have you been reborn and renewed by the Holy Spirit? (If you are not sure, call your pastor or group leader this week and discuss your questions and concerns.) This is the only way to be free from the sin of envy in your life. How is envy separating you from others?

_____

_____

_____

_____

_____

_____

_____

DEVOTIONALS

DAY 5

It's MY Way or the Highway

What causes fights and quarrels among you? Don't they come from your desires that battle within you? You want something but don't get it. You kill and covet, but you cannot have what you want. You quarrel and fight. You do not have, because you do not ask God. When you ask, you do not receive, because you ask with wrong motives, that you may spend what you get on your pleasures (James 4:1-3).

If you stop to analyze most quarrels, you will find that they start with a basic case of the "I wants." We think we need something, whether it is money, possessions, the meeting of an emotional need, or anything else. When we don't get what we think we deserve, we get mad. It makes us cranky, and we start to pick at others. Sometimes we pick on the person we think is to blame for our needs going unmet. But sometimes we pick on an innocent bystander.

Part of our problem is the fact that we don't ask God to meet our needs. Then when we do, we act like a spoiled brat: "Give me what I want, or else!" When He doesn't respond, we think He doesn't care. We don't trust God to know or care about what is best for us. We have "Number One" in the center again.

God will never refuse us good things just to be mean. He wants us to ask Him for what we need, but He doesn't respond to our requests like a penny gumball machine. He only gives us what will be good for us.

What do you most want now that you are not receiving? Could it be that God knows it's not best for you? How can you begin to trust God more with that desire and understand His plan for your life?

_____

_____

_____

_____

_____

_____

_____

_____

DEVOTIONALS

DAY 6

The Real Wise Guys

Who is wise and understanding among you? Let him show it by his good life, by deeds done in the humility that comes from wisdom. But if you harbor bitter envy and selfish ambition in your hearts, do not boast about it or deny the truth. Such "wisdom" does not come down from heaven but is earthly, unspiritual, of the devil. For where you have envy and selfish ambition, there you find disorder and every evil practice (James 3:13-16).

According to worldly wisdom, selfish ambition is a great motive. "If you don't look out for yourself, no one else will." "It's a dog eat dog world." "Envying others gives you the drive to succeed. With enough ambition, envy, and ruthlessness, you can be on the top of the heap." What more could you want? Actually, this "wisdom" is straight from the devil. Envy and selfish ambition may push you higher up the ladder. But at what cost? How many people made in God's image will you crush on the way? How much turmoil, dissension, and hatred will you stir up?

What kind of wisdom are you showing in your life? How can you gain godly wisdom instead of worldly wisdom?

_____

_____

_____

_____

_____

_____

_____

_____

_____

_____

_____

_____

_____

DEVOTIONALS

DAY 7

Make A Clean Sweep

Therefore, rid yourselves of all malice and all deceit, hypocrisy, envy, and slander of every kind. Like newborn babies, crave pure spiritual milk, so that by it you may grow up in your salvation, now that you have tasted that the Lord is good (1 Peter 2:1-3).

Peter has such a great way of simplifying this. He essentially says, "Get rid of sin." Sounds easy, right? We can all testify to the fact that it doesn't feel that simple in real life. So why does God often answer the problem of sin with the order to dump it? Because having that mindset is the first step to changing our ways. We may well struggle to actually dig all of the sin out of our lives and untangle ourselves from its grasp, but we have to start with the attitude that says, "Get rid of it." We can't leave a mental loophole that says, "Unless it gets too hard," or "I'll deal with it later," or "It's not so bad." We have to start out with the clean-sweep mentality.

Once we have the right attitude, then we have to replace those old ways with what Peter calls "pure spiritual milk." Hebrews 5:12-13 refers to this spiritual milk as the baby food of the Christian life. This is the beginner stuff, the elementary teachings about Christ. As we begin to follow Christ, we exchange our selfish ambitions for the ambition to be like Him. As we understand who He is, why He had to die, and how much He loves us, the envy and evil will be pushed aside to make room for better things. Have you ever seen the way a hungry baby goes after milk? It seems that all a baby does is eat and grow. We should crave knowledge of Christ, fill our minds and hearts with it, taste of God, and know that He is good. Then we will grow up in our salvation and be ready for the hard stuff that will come our way.

Do you have a consuming hunger to know God? Why or why not? (Consider taking some time today to read the third chapter of John, and pick a verse to memorize.)

_____

_____

_____

_____

_____

_____

DEVOTIONALS

DAY 8

Envy's Antidote

Be devoted to one another in brotherly love. Honor one another above yourselves (Romans 12:10).

When a poisonous snake bites someone, the doctors will give that person an antidote for the poison. The antidote neutralizes the action of the snake's venom, and keeps the person from dying. Envy is like a poisonous snake to our spiritual lives. It will inject its bitter venom and eventually make us ineffective—unhappy, unproductive, and destructive to others. Envy is a serious poison.

The antidote to the poison of envy is an attitude of love and humility. Instead of selfishly thinking of our own desires, God wants us to be caring and considerate of others. This isn't something that we can manufacture on our own. Only the power of God at work in our hearts will make us able to put envy's antidote into practice.

What are some practical ways you could show love and humility to people in your life right now?

_____

_____

_____

_____

_____

_____

_____

_____

_____

_____

_____

DEVOTIONALS

DAY 9

Turning the Tables

Rejoice with those who rejoice; mourn with those who mourn (Romans 12:15).

When we envy others, we can't be glad for the blessings in their lives. If we can't have the things we want, we don't want anyone else to have them either. Envy is grouchy when others are blessed, and gloats when their misfortunes bring them down. This isn't God's way, and it isn't His plan for His children either. When we find ourselves dissatisfied and wishing that we could have what God has given to someone else, then it is time to turn the tables on ourselves.

Self has to come last, and sympathy for others first. When others are blessed, we are to be happy for them, even if we are miserable ourselves. When others are experiencing sorrow, we are to comfort them and be sorry for their pain, even if we thought they brought it on themselves. God wants us to be tenderhearted toward one another, loving and caring. There is no room for envy in God's system.

Read 1 Corinthians 13. Now read it again, replacing the word "love" with your own name. How do you measure up? What does this tell you about the areas you need to work on in order to love God's way?

_____

_____

_____

_____

_____

_____

_____

_____

_____

_____

_____

_____

DEVOTIONALS

DAY 10

Real Satisfaction

Satisfy us in the morning with your unfailing love, that we may sing for joy and be glad all our days (Psalm 90:14).

Envy really comes from a basic dissatisfaction. We have the lingering feeling that God is trying to deprive us of something, and that He treats other people better than He treats us. As long as we are not satisfied with who God is and what He gives us, we are going to struggle with envying other people. Even when we get the things we envied, we won't feel content. Someone else will always have something better. There is always something else to want, something else about which to feel dissatisfied. The only One who can give us real satisfaction is God.

Are you relaxed and at peace with God, or are you restless and dissatisfied? Stop to analyze your dissatisfaction. Where is this coming from? What are you going to do about it?

_____

_____

_____

_____

_____

_____

_____

_____

_____

_____

_____

_____

_____

_____

SMALL-GROUP SESSION

Escape the Ugly Green Monster of Envy

Proverbs 14:30; Philippians 4:11-13; James 3:16;
1 Corinthians 13:4; James 5:16; Romans 12:15

Envy is as "ugly as sin" because it is sin. In a way, each fatal distraction is the opposite of a special virtue. For example, pride opposes humility. Anger opposes self-control and forgiveness. Envy opposes contentment and love for others. The first two fatal distractions we've talked about begin with some pleasure. It is kind of fun to stick out our chests and become elevated with pride. It is exciting to have that rush of adrenalin when we spew our hot lava of anger all over someone. Envy is different. Right from the starting block it involves anguish, turmoil, and problems. Envy is just plain ugly.

START IT UP

Wanting what others have comes so naturally for us. From the time children begin talking, it seems that the chant "Mine. Mine. Mine!" is a favorite.

1. When you were in grade school, what did other kids have that made you green with envy?

2. If you got what you wanted, did it live up to your expectations?

TALK IT UP

Before we can continue with this study on envy, we have to define what it is. Envy is being sad over others' successes and a fan of their failures. It causes us to want someone else's good thing for ourselves. Envy wants everyone else to be as unhappy or unsuccessful as we are. It is the great leveler. If it can't level us up, it tries to level others down.

So What's the Big Deal?

Some of us are saying right now, "A little envy is not such a big deal. I can want what someone else has without it being such a big problem. It is a minor sin." Think again. There is no such thing as a minor sin. God is not some disorganized deity who arbitrarily came up with a grocery list of things that He decided to call sins. When God says something is sin, it is because it is contrary to His character. It is something that will obstruct our relationship with Him. It is something that will damage us and damage others. God doesn't call envy "sin" just to be mean. He told us that envy is sin because He loves us and wants us to have the chance to live life rightly. He wants us to have a change of heart and love others with His love. And love does not leave room for envy.

Read Proverbs 14:30

Envy really does matter. It is listed in the New Testament with some ugly counterparts like deceit, rudeness, murder, drunkenness, orgies, hypocrisy, slander, and stealing. No one would say all these are "little sins" that don't really matter.

3. What kinds of rottenness can envy bring into the lives of people?

Envy's Ugly Tongue

Envy has four ugly facets that will appear in our lives if it is left unchecked. First, it will produce *plastic praise*. Envy is rooted in a certain kind of self-centeredness that we call "poor self-esteem." When we have poor self-esteem, we are always thinking that we don't measure up. As a result, we try to make up for what we

lack by being the strongest, the fastest, the leanest, and the meanest. We feel bad about ourselves, and we try to make ourselves feel better by belittling those we actually envy. We give plastic praise—a word of praise, balanced with a belittling statement. "She is a super mom, but you should see her house—it's like a pigsty!" Plastic praise is used to camouflage inferiority, and it is fueled by envy.

Envy also causes us to *slander* people. When we envy someone's possessions, beauty, or charisma, we slander them in order to make their accomplishments look smaller. We start to assume mean motives in others because we envy them.

Condescending comparisons or one-upmanship also come from envy. Envy makes us unable to rejoice with another person's joy. Whenever someone tells us about an accomplishment, we refuse to be impressed; we always have to top their story with our own bigger and better story.

Gossip has become elevated to a form of entertainment. Have you ever wondered why the tabloid TV shows and the gossip columns are so popular? It is partly because of envy. We love to read about the dirty laundry of celebrities because it makes us feel superior. Envy takes pleasure in the problems of others.

Envy's Ugly Core

Envy is directly linked to lack of contentment. If we constantly want what others have, how can we find contentment?

Read Philippians 4:11-13

This word "contentment" does not imply compliancy or apathy; it means, "being happy with what you have or what you are." Envy is the opposite of contentment. Envy makes us look at what other people have and compare it unfavorably with what we have. Contentment is looking at who God is and realizing that anything we need He is both willing and able to supply.

4. Does being content with what we have mean that we should not work to make things better for ourselves? How should we balance ambition and contentment?

5. What is the "secret" of contentment that Paul mentions?

Envy's Ugly Produce

Read James 3:16; 1 Corinthians 13:4

It's an interesting fact that we tend to be envious of our peers. Saul envied David, not because of his harp or because he was handsome. He was jealous of David's military and leadership qualities. He was jealous because he was afraid David would take his place. It is the same with us. A surgeon is jealous of another surgeon, not of a chef. A chef is envious of another chef, not of a groundskeeper.

This is really unfortunate because our peers can provide some of the best friendships we have because of the common interests and goals we share.

6. What are some ways you have seen envy separate you and your peers?

7. How are love and envy opposed to one another? How can you reach out with love to those who are separated from you because of envy?

Desire the Best Things

We have seen how ugly envy is and how it produces ugly fruit. But our situation isn't hopeless. We can get rid of the sin of envy. The following three guidelines will help us to overcome this fatal distraction.

Read James 5:16

The first thing we have to do is come clean about our sins. We have to admit that we are having feelings of envy, and we have to ask God for help. Most of the time, we try to disguise these feelings. We keep them hidden in the dark corners of our souls and do not question why we do what we do. The only way we can get rid of envy is to drag it out into the light of day. We have to confess our sin and say,

"God, I have a problem with envy." This is where our trusted Christian friends come in. We need the encouragement of a loving friend who will pray for us and keep on loving us even though we aren't perfect.

8. What does it take to feel safe with this level of vulnerability? Do you have someone you could talk to like this?

Read Romans 12:15

Second, we need to develop an attitude of gratitude. Envy rejoices when others weep and weeps when others rejoice. Instead, we need to celebrate when good things happen to other people and sympathize when they face hardships. We shouldn't compare our lot with others. We should thank God for the blessings He gives to us – and to others.

9. How can you thank God when you don't feel thankful? Is it dishonest to say thanks when you feel the opposite way?

Third, we must learn to anticipate envy. We can't just say, "I will rejoice with others from now on" and live an envy-free life forever. Envy will keep popping up its ugly green head, and we have to be ready to smack it. Certain things trigger envy in each of us. Anticipate your envy triggers and learn to stay away from them. If you are in a position where you can't keep away from a situation that causes you to be envious, pray for God's protection before you enter it. When you are in the envy-strike-zone, it's too late to put on your armor. You must prepare ahead of time.

LIFT IT UP

Envy involves the pursuit of things like prestige, power, and significance, which means there is really only one cure. We have to oppose envy and pursue God. We have to become fully devoted followers of Christ. Many of us here would say that God is important to us, but He is important in the midst of other important things. For some of us, He is just an extracurricular activity. Others of us have been

inoculated with a mild form of Christianity so that we won't catch the real disease. But God says, "Pursue Me." If we pursue God, we are pursuing something bigger and better than someone else's house, car, money, or career. When we pursue God and focus on Him, other things don't mean much anymore. They lose their luster.

"Since we live by the Spirit, let us keep in step with the Spirit. Let us not become conceited, provoking and envying each other" (Galatians 5:25-26).

10. How high on your "pursuit list" is the pursuit of God? If you realize that He is really not number one, what do you think is? Is it really worth it?

11. In what areas do you struggle with envy? What will you do in the coming week to overcome it? How can this group pray for you?

Take time to pray specifically for each other in those areas where you would like to oppose envy and pursue God.

My Prayer Needs:

_____

_____

_____

My Group's Prayer Needs:

Leila's ~ Ashley/Brandon's girlfriend ~ Lesion check for cancer

Mrs. Kelley ~ Husband passed away

Sister Leslie - Friend committed suicide. - Watkins family

Debbie - Brother in Iraq / Dad + Stepbrother - traveling - mission work

_____

_____

_____

_____

DEVOTIONALS

DAY 1

Just Nothing

As a door turns on its hinges, so a sluggard turns on his bed. The sluggard buries his hand in the dish; he is too lazy to bring it back to his mouth (Proverbs 26:14-15).

The author of Proverbs paints us a couple of vivid word pictures here. Just imagine it: this person reaches into the potato chip bag, but it takes too much effort to take his hand back out again. One imagines the sluggard sitting with mouth half-open, eyes focused on nothing, the mind a blank. This isn't a case of mental deficiency. This is a case of character deficiency.

The Bible, particularly the Book of Proverbs, has quite a lot to say about what will happen to those who develop laziness to a high art. A sluggard is a person completely dominated by a sin called slothfulness. In ordinary language, slothfulness is basic, serious laziness. Unlike some sins, which involve doing wrong actions, slothfulness is the sin of doing nothing. That's right—just nothing. Nothing bad and nothing good either. People with this fatal distraction do nothing to hurt someone else and nothing to help someone who is in need right before their eyes. They simply do nothing.

Has it occurred to you that overt disobedience isn't the only kind of sin? In what areas might you be guilty of sinning by doing nothing? Spend some time today thinking about this.

_____

_____

_____

_____

_____

_____

_____

_____

_____

_____

DEVOTIONALS

DAY 2

Paying the Bills—Plus Interest

The way of the sluggard is blocked with thorns, but the path of the upright is a highway (Proverbs 15:19).

The whole goal of a lazy person is to avoid effort. A sluggard or sloth always looks for the path of least resistance. The best way sometimes looks too painful or too difficult, so we avoid it, doing something easier instead. At the time, this may seem like the easiest path to take because it takes effort to think and plan. Actually, when we are slothful, we are shooting ourselves in the foot. The longer we let things slide, the harder our lives will be in the future. God always blesses those who act uprightly. It won't be easy at the time, but it always saves future trouble. If we are truly motivated to avoid problems, we will deal with them when they first show up and are still small and easy to handle.

What chores do you tend to put off doing? What problems in your relationships do you tend to ignore? Is there something that you need to mend now, before it gets any worse?

_____

_____

_____

_____

_____

_____

_____

_____

_____

_____

_____

DEVOTIONALS

DAY 3

Excuses, Excuses

The sluggard says, "There is a lion outside!" or, "I will be murdered in the streets!"
(Proverbs 22:13).

A slothful person is really good at coming up with excuses. We can make ourselves sound so responsible, so caring, so sincere when all the time our real motives are simple laziness. "I would help you, but I just don't want to put my family in danger." "I would stop by, but I might catch the disease too." Sometimes fear motivates these excuses, but often we are excusing ourselves from effort, not danger. We just don't want to deal with the inconvenience. The sad thing is that when we excuse ourselves from effort, we are also excusing ourselves from blessing.

What excuses have you used recently to keep from doing something that disturbed your comfort? What do you think your real motive was?

_____

_____

_____

_____

_____

_____

_____

_____

_____

_____

_____

_____

_____

_____

DEVOTIONALS

DAY 4

Hey! Wake Up!

I went past the field of the sluggard, past the vineyard of the man who lacks judgment; thorns had come up everywhere, the ground was covered with weeds, and the stone wall was in ruins. I applied my heart to what I observed and learned a lesson from what I saw: A little sleep, a little slumber, a little folding of the hands to rest—and poverty will come on you like a bandit and scarcity like an armed man (Proverbs 24:30-34).

Have you ever heard of the Law of Entropy? Even if we don't recall its name, we know it well. Entropy is the general trend of the universe toward disorder. What happens when you clean the house perfectly, and then sit back with your feet up for a few days? You said it. It looks like a whirlwind went through. In spite of a lifetime of experience with entropy, we don't really believe in it. We still somehow think that everything will stay the same until we get around to dealing with it. We don't realize that the time will come when things have gone too far, when our chance is over. Weeds will take over the vineyard. The house will fall down around us. The relationship will die. The opportunity to serve will pass. The hurting person will languish. Just because we did nothing, does not mean nothing happened.

Where is entropy taking over in your life? What action do you need to take to bring back order?

_____

_____

_____

_____

_____

_____

_____

_____

_____

_____

_____

_____

_____

DEVOTIONALS

DAY 5

It Takes Patience

We do not want you to become lazy, but to imitate those who through faith and patience inherit what has been promised (Hebrews 6:12).

Slothfulness is one of the faces of impatience. Some people who lack patience grow frustrated and angry. Some just lie down and quit when things start to get hard. If something isn't easy the first time, the sloth doesn't bother to keep trying. If the answer doesn't come through instantly, he quits praying. If he can't get rid of a sin on the first try, he doesn't bother any more. This isn't what God has called us to be. Instead, He has called us to strive for faith and patience. Faith believes that God is working, even when we can't see it. Patience believes that His solution and His timing will be perfect.

Identify one area of your spiritual life where laziness has taken over. Is it prayer? Is it Scripture reading? Is it ministry? Something else? What can you do to change this?

DEVOTIONALS

DAY 6

Get Up and Run

Therefore, since we are surrounded by such a great cloud of witnesses, let us throw off everything that hinders and the sin that so easily entangles, and let us run with perseverance the race marked out for us (Hebrews 12:1).

Following Christ isn't a ride in a recliner. It is a race. We often think that once we have believed we can just sit back and let the world roll by. Our troubles are over, nothing bad will ever happen again. From now on, it's all God's deal. This is completely true in the sense that Jesus' death paid for our sins once and for all. We can do nothing to earn our way into God's favor. Christ's blood paid the full price, there is nothing to add. But He didn't save us to leave us like we are. We have been reborn into God's family, and we don't have the option of going back to the way we were. We don't fit in any longer. The Holy Spirit in us won't let us continue to enjoy sin. If we are going to live the life God meant for us, we must throw off the old ways, and run for all we are worth.

What weights are entangling you and hindering you from running your race and following God's plan for your life?

_____

_____

_____

_____

_____

_____

_____

_____

_____

_____

_____

_____

DEVOTIONALS

DAY 7

Encouragement from Christ's Example

Let us fix our eyes on Jesus, the author and perfecter of our faith, who for the joy set before him endured the cross, scorning its shame, and sat down at the right hand of the throne of God. Consider him who endured such opposition from sinful men, so that you will not grow weary and lose heart (Hebrews 12:2-3).

God knows that there will be times when we will grow tired of the struggle. Getting up and going one more time just seems like too much. All we want to do is lie down and go to sleep for about a hundred years. We don't want to think about resisting our sins or battling the strongholds in our lives anymore. For just a little while, we don't want to have to care. When we start feeling this way, we need to turn our thoughts to Jesus.

God isn't some far-off deity who cannot understand your struggles. He became a human, and He suffered and died for your sake so that you could be free. When you become weary with doing good, remember that He understands and be encouraged. He who endured to the end will help you to endure as well.

What is an area in your life where you are growing weary? How does Jesus inspire you to keep going? How can the joy of eternity in heaven keep you motivated?

_____

_____

_____

_____

_____

_____

_____

_____

_____

DEVOTIONALS

DAY 8

Drawing Blood

In your struggle against sin, you have not yet resisted to the point of shedding your blood (Hebrews 12:4).

When we are steeped in slothfulness, the thought of resisting anything is almost exhausting. We don't even think about resisting to the point of shedding our blood. Think about this for a minute. How seriously do you really take sin in your life? If you were in the death grip of a murderous ruffian, wouldn't you fight tooth and nail to get free? You wouldn't worry about losing a little blood; you'd be too concerned about your life. We should be looking at sin in the same way. It is very serious, and is something that we must fight tooth and nail to escape.

How far are you willing to go to resist sin? Would you shed blood over it? Or is a feeble "leave me alone" as far as you ever get? How should your attitudes toward sin change?

DEVOTIONALS

DAY 9

The Goal

I press on toward the goal to win the prize for which God has called me heavenward in Christ Jesus (Philippians 3:14).

Have you ever gone on a walk for no particular reason, to no particular place? There is no motivation to walk fast. If you get tired, you can just stop. It can be very relaxing. But it can also feel pointless. You probably won't go very far, and you certainly won't press on when you get tired.

God hasn't given us a pointless race to run. We aren't jogging along, wondering where we are going and what the point of it all is. We have a goal, and it is a goal that is worth pressing on toward. At the end of our lives, we are going to meet Jesus face to face. We are finally going to see the One who gave His life for us. We'll be able to touch Him, and then we'll understand everything that's been puzzling us. He is the prize, the goal, the finish line. He will be worth it all!

When you first start following Christ, He may seem very far off, and a little unreal. But if you keep your eyes fixed on the goal, He will come into focus. Think about the finish line. Do you want to meet Jesus while running toward Him, or while you're sitting by the roadside doing nothing?

_____

_____

_____

_____

_____

_____

_____

_____

_____

_____

_____

DEVOTIONALS

DAY 10

Moving On

Through these he has given us his very great and precious promises, so that through them you may participate in the divine nature and escape the corruption in the world caused by evil desires. For this very reason, make every effort to add to your faith goodness; and to goodness, knowledge; and to knowledge, self-control; and to self-control, perseverance; and to perseverance, godliness; and to godliness, brotherly kindness; and to brotherly kindness, love. For if you possess these qualities in increasing measure, they will keep you from being ineffective and unproductive in your knowledge of our Lord Jesus Christ (2 Peter 1:4-8).

A slothful person is the perfect example of one who is ineffective and unproductive. Obviously, doing nothing gets nothing done. Read this passage again carefully. Notice all of the active terms used: "participate," "escape," "make every effort," "add," "increasing measure." It's easier to let things slide, for just another day or two. But, don't do it. Start now to "add to your faith goodness; and to goodness knowledge ... self-control ... perseverance ... godliness ... brotherly kindness ... and love." It won't always be easy, but it will be worth it. Godliness and slothfulness don't work together. One or the other will fall by the wayside.

The question is, which do you choose today: godliness or slothfulness? What can you do in the coming week to become more effective and productive for Christ?

_____

_____

_____

_____

_____

_____

_____

_____

_____

_____

Stop the Sloth from Hanging Around

Matthew 25:1-46; Mark 14:32-42; 1 Peter 5:8-10

A fascinating creature lives in the jungles of South America. It is a slow-moving, toothless tree-dweller that hangs by its claws for days at a time while it does absolutely nothing. This animal is called the sloth.

Sadly, this is not only a description of a South-American mammal. It is a description of each one of us at one time or another.

START IT UP

Slothfulness isn't a very nice word. No one would want to be described as slothful; it just sounds bad. The Bible tells us that it is bad because being slothful has serious implications and consequences. Let's find out what slothfulness really is and how we can face this fatal distraction and overcome it.

1.   What is your favorite form of relaxation?

2.   Do you see yourself as more of a go-getter or are you a procrastinator? What activities are you most likely to put off until "later"?

TALK IT UP

God laid out in His Word a list of attitudes and behaviors known as sins. God didn't come up with this list by asking for a vote from all the humans on earth. He didn't compile statistics and take polls. He measured sin against His own perfect and righteous character. The things that God calls sin will damage our lives, the lives of others, and our relationship with Him.

We could say that there are basically two kinds of sins—sins of commission and sins of omission. Sins of commission are pretty obvious. They are those things we do that are against God's directives. Sins of omission aren't quite so easy. These are the things we should have and could have done, but failed to do. Slothfulness is the perfect example of a sin of omission. In fact, it is the root beneath many of our sins of omission.

What Jesus Said About Slothfulness

Jesus had a lot to say about slothfulness, and at one time He told His disciples three parables to illustrate the problems that can result from this fatal distraction.

Read Matthew 25:1-13 "The Parable of the Ten Virgins"

3. What do you think the different people and things in this parable represent? Why couldn't the wise virgins share their oil with the foolish virgins?

Read Matthew 25:14-30 "The Parable of the Talents"

4. How can Christ-followers multiply their "talents" for the Master? How might you be burying your talent?

Read Matthew 25:31-46 "The Sheep and the Goats"

5. What do these parables tell you about the seriousness of slothfulness?

Even though many of us may clean house immaculately, compete vigorously, and work strategically, we can still be stranded in sloth. Sloth does not pop up everywhere. It is selective. If we look at our lives today, we will see this slow-moving, toothless mentality hanging from some surprising areas of our life.

What Slothfulness Looks Like

Typically, we think that a sloth is someone who won't work, who lies around on the couch drinking beer and watching soap operas while the house goes to ruin and the kids run wild in the streets. We imagine a sloth in dirty clothes, living in a mess of dirty dishes, candy wrappers, old newspapers, and dead TV remotes. In fact, slothfulness is a lot more subtle than we think. In our workaholic, tense culture, we don't often see a "typical" sloth. But that doesn't mean sloths don't exist.

Read Mark 14:32-42

Why is slothfulness considered to be a fatal distraction? First, slothfulness can make us *too lethargic to love*. Love is a choice that we make to reach out to another, regardless of how we feel. We don't have to be reminded that love is not all roses and kisses. There are times when it takes a lot of work to love, times when we don't feel loving, and times when we are just too tired to bother. That is where sloth comes in. Slothfulness takes the easy way, just sitting back, and letting the opportunities slide by. You may say, "I'm just not in love anymore. Love is not flowing." Love should not be based on emotions. It is a decision of the will. Jesus' disciples had a perfect opportunity to demonstrate love for Him, but they chose to sleep instead. Are we going to pass up opportunities to love and encourage those who are close to us, just because we are sleepy, tired, or cranky?

Second, sloth can make us *too sluggish to stand*. Jesus told Peter to watch and pray so that he would not fall into temptation. He didn't say to watch once and pray once. He said watch and pray continually. We have to practice saying "no" to

ourselves. If we say "yes" to every impulse, we are not going to be able to say no when temptation comes our way.

Sloth has another seductive side. It can make us *too mellow to move*. Jesus looked at His disciples sleeping and said, "The spirit is willing, but the body is weak" (Mark 14:38). He knew that the disciples weren't saying, "No way, I don't care what happens to you. I refuse to stay awake." Their hearts were willing, but when it came right down to the crunch of actually getting up and moving, they didn't do it. They didn't push pass their physical tiredness to do what they really wanted to do.

6. Can you connect to any of these signs of slothfulness? Give an example of how and where these signs may be evident in your life.

How to Guard Against Slothfulness

Read 1 Peter 5:8-10

If you watch a predator hunt, you will notice that it looks for a weak animal, a sluggish animal, or an animal that is not paying attention. Dealing with sin takes an alert mind and an attitude of action. If we sit back and don't bother to look around, sin will be at our throats. Satan is real, he is a predator, and he is out to get us. We can't turn our backs for a moment.

Some of us get involved in slothful supplication. We pray one time to be delivered from a problem with which we are dealing. Then we check it off our list and say, "There, that's God's job now." We think that God will suddenly deliver us, and we will have no desire for that particular temptation again. This is a sloppy and slothful supplication. Dealing with sin is a continual battle. We will never be able to sit back and say, "That is conquered once and for all." We have to stay on our guard. If we become sluggish, sin will be there ripping us apart before we know what is happening.

The good news is that the more we use our muscles of resistance, the stronger they will become. The more we practice alertness, the better able we will be to see the temptations coming.

7.   When Satan looks at you, what areas of vulnerability does he see?

8.   What can you actively do to strengthen these areas of weakness?

LIFT IT UP

When Jesus came back the third time to find His disciples sleeping, He said, "Are you still sleeping and resting? Enough! The hour has come. Look, the Son of Man is betrayed into the hands of sinners" (Mark 14:41). In other words, they had missed it. They had the chance to minister to Jesus, to lighten His hardest hour by sharing it, and they missed it.

That's the way slothfulness works. We lay back, thinking, "I just can't move right now. I am too tired. This is too comfortable." We think there will be another chance later, when it is more convenient. We don't realize that it can be too late if we wait.

Remember the sheep and the goats? The goats didn't realize that their big sin was a sin of omission. They were probably going about their lives saying, "I'm a pretty good guy. I don't hurt anybody. I don't cause problems for other people." But they missed their chance to serve God. They missed their chance to serve Him and other people. We don't have a very good concept of how short life is. The few years we have on this earth are the only chance we will ever have to serve others, the only chance we will ever have to build others up, to love them, and to influence them for the kingdom of God. If we blow this chance, there is no other.

9.   What slothful attitudes do you have in your life? Are you slothful in your relationships? In recognizing temptation or sin? In serving others? In prayer?

10. What practical action can you take this week to change one of these things?

Take time to pray specifically for each other in those areas where slothfulness is a struggle.

My Prayer Needs:

_____

_____

_____

_____

_____

_____

My Group's Prayer Needs:

Debbie - traveling - picking up girls

Jan - Danny Duke + Hospital

Brandy surgery - daughter -

Susan Wall + surgery on feet - May - may have to amputate

Bruce Watson - physical pain from accident

Jeff - sleep disorder

Lori - looking for new job

Painter -

DEVOTIONALS

DAY 1

Run for Your Life

Flee from sexual immorality. All other sins a man commits are outside his body, but he who sins sexually sins against his own body (1 Corinthians 6:18).

Flee—that means we turn tail and run as fast as we can. God didn't tell us to toughen ourselves to sexual immorality, to stay and fight it, or to learn to handle it better. He said that there is only one way to deal with it—we have to run.

Sex in and of itself is not sinful. God designed it to be beautiful and pleasurable. But, sex has a certain mysterious quality. It binds two people together physically, emotionally, and spiritually. This intimate act is part of what makes marriage a special, unique relationship—it unites two people as one. Because of this quality, sexual sin is particularly devastating. It affects the whole person, both spirit and body. It affects the emotions and it affects relationships. Any time sexual intimacy is engaged in outside of the marriage relationship—outside of one man and one woman who are committed to each other for life—it will result in damage. God says that we are not to mess around with it for even a second. The only way to stay clean is to run for our lives.

Is there something in your life—a time, a place, an activity—that makes you more vulnerable to this temptation? What do you need to do to overcome it?

_____

_____

_____

_____

_____

_____

_____

_____

_____

_____

_____

_____

DEVOTIONALS

DAY 2

The Heart of the Issue

You have heard that it was said, "Do not commit adultery." But I tell you that anyone who looks at a woman lustfully has already committed adultery with her in his heart (Matthew 5:27-28).

What did God say about dealing with sexual immorality? He said, "Flee." He drew a clear line in the sand —no sex outside of marriage. Period. Great, we can handle that. However, Jesus is now taking us a step further. As usual, He is going beyond actions to the heart issues. If you were running from a wild beast, an enemy that you knew was too strong for you; would you flirt with danger by stopping every now and then to let it catch up with you? Would you be entertained by watching it devour others? Of course not! If you behaved like that, the wild beast would devour you too. What makes you think that we will be any stronger when it comes to lust and sexual immorality? Fleeing from immorality must begin with fleeing from lust. Every affair, every sexual sin, begins with lustful thinking. It is the first step in sexual sin because it involves our heart, which ultimately leads us to action.

Even if you have never physically sinned sexually, your heart may be guilty. Have you confessed your internal unseen sins to God and asked Him to give you the desire and power to turn away from lust when it comes?

_____

_____

_____

_____

_____

_____

_____

_____

_____

_____

_____

_____

DEVOTIONALS

DAY 3

Lust-buster #1:

Refrain from flirtatious comments and gestures.

Can a man scoop fire into his lap without his clothes being burned? Can a man walk on hot coals without his feet being scorched? (Proverbs 6:27-28).

In order to effectively deal with the sin of lust in our lives, we need to get a handle on some strategies for avoiding situations that will bring those feelings up. In the next several devotionals, we will look at five different lust-busters to help us in our struggles with this fatal distraction.

Sometimes you will meet a person who seems to know only one way to relate to the opposite sex. This kind of person automatically makes flirtatious comments or acts in a flirtatious manner. People like this do not see the harm in what they are doing. They think it is a viable style of relating to others.

Some may say, "But I am just a huggy, touchy kind of person. It is no big deal to me. I don't have any wrong motives. I just have a really outgoing personality." Yes, that particular person might be innocent. But what about the other person? Do you ever stop to think that your actions might be a lure for someone else? Do you know how quickly an "innocent" flirtatious conversation can lead down the road to lust and sexual sin? We are responsible to not put stumbling blocks in the way of others. This is a great opportunity to serve others by putting their best interests ahead of our own.

What are some ways that you relate to people of the opposite sex that could be adding a sexual or flirtatious overtone to the conversation? What might you need to change in the way you interact with other people?

_____

_____

_____

_____

_____

_____

DEVOTIONALS

DAY 4

Lust-buster #2:

Look past the lure of lust to the consequences.

Then, after desire has conceived, it gives birth to sin; and sin, when it is full-grown, gives birth to death (James 1:15).

When we are following the lure of lust, we are injected with a dose of forgetfulness. We forget God. We forget the presence of the Holy Spirit. We just focus on the lure and not the consequences.

According to James, lust does not end with itself. We cannot enjoy lustful thoughts, and expect it to end there. "After desire has conceived," that is, as soon as we give it houseroom, as soon as we entertain it for even just a few minutes, "it gives birth to sin."

Read Joseph's story in Genesis 39:5-12.

Joseph is an example of one man who looked ahead to the consequences of lust. He saw the lure, and he saw what would be ahead. Did you notice what he did? He did not try to reason with Mrs. Potiphar. He did not say, "Well, it won't hurt me just to look." He did not say, "She is so lonely, she just needs me to be nice to her." It says that Joseph "left his cloak in her hand and ran." When we are running, we won't succumb to the lure of lust.

What are the short and long-term consequences of letting lust live in your life? How can you refocus on future consequences?

_____

_____

_____

_____

_____

_____

_____

DEVOTIONALS

DAY 5

Lust-buster #3:

Monitor your media intake.

I made a covenant with my eyes not to look lustfully at a girl. … Does he not see my ways and count my every step? (Job 31:1,4).

Let's get real. Hundreds and hundreds of sexually suggestive messages bombard us day in and day out. Our culture spends billions of dollars each year on pornography, strip clubs, and other sexually explicit material. It is out there, and it is very easy to obtain.

Job didn't say that he was going to make a covenant later, when temptation started. He didn't wait for the lure of lust to begin. He made the covenant first. In other words, we are to put a filter over our minds. This filter should have Philippians 4:8 written on it. "Whatever is true, whatever is noble, whatever is right, whatever is pure, whatever is lovely, whatever is admirable—if anything is excellent or praiseworthy—think about such things."

The only way we can handle the lure of lust is to flee and run from temptation. That includes running from certain movies, magazines, TV shows, and novels.

You may be saying, "Well, this movie only has a couple of suggestive parts. I can handle it. A little bit of sin is not going to affect me." Hey, who are you trying to kid? One little explicit scene can feed lust in your life for weeks. Don't overestimate what you can handle. "Just a little bit" of lustful thinking wears away at our protective barriers so gradually that we don't even notice it.

As you apply Philippians 4:8, in what ways might your media intake need to be changed? What does it make you think when you realize that God watches every little thing you do and think?

_____

_____

_____

_____

_____

DEVOTIONALS

DAY 6

Lust-buster #4:

Maximize your sexual relationship within your marriage.

Do not deprive each other except by mutual consent and for a time, so that you may devote yourselves to prayer. Then come together again so that Satan will not tempt you because of your lack of self-control (1 Corinthians 7:5).

Some people seem to think that once they are married, sexual temptation will end. They will no longer have to flee the lure of lust. Because of this kind of thinking, they will often sit back and let things slide. They don't put enough time and energy into their marriages. They don't avoid situations of temptation, and then they are surprised when they fall into sin. They wonder how they got so far away from God, how they ended up committing adultery, and how they destroyed their marriages.

Married couples are supposed to be on the alert to keep one another satisfied. When each spouse has the attitude of loving and giving, of doing all he or she can to meet the needs of the other person, there is room to abstain briefly for the right reasons. But do not let it be for too long. It is not right to create situations that make your spouse more vulnerable to temptation.

The biblical "math of marriage" is one plus one equals one. Married couples are to seek this sense of oneness, beginning with common faith in Jesus Christ. God invented the sexual relationship between a husband and wife. He means for it to be beautiful and pleasurable. It is the thermometer that suggests how well we are growing in the oneness that defines a good marriage.

What are some things that you and your spouse could do to better meet one another's needs for romance and intimacy?

_____

_____

_____

_____

_____

_____

DEVOTIONALS

DAY 7

Lust-buster #5:

Establish accountability in your life.

As iron sharpens iron, so one man sharpens another (Proverbs 27:17).

We each need someone in our lives who knows us very well and loves us for who we are— someone with whom we can talk about our temptations. This person cannot be someone who tells off-color jokes, brags about sexual conquests, recklessly flirts with others, or gawks at members of the opposite sex. Run from those people. We need to have a friend who knows Christ personally, and who will encourage us to live a pure life.

Establishing accountability can be difficult. It is sometimes hard to be that open with another person. It can be hard to confess our failures or to take a justified rebuke, but it will be worth it in the end.

Do you have someone who can fill this place in your life? If not, ask God to send you a close friend who can "sharpen" you. Write down some names of potential accountability partners in the space below.

_____

_____

_____

_____

_____

_____

_____

_____

_____

_____

_____

_____

_____

DEVOTIONALS

DAY 8

Chasing Off the Enemy

Submit yourselves, then, to God. Resist the devil, and he will flee from you (James 4:7).

Many times, it seems that Satan is just out to get us. We will be going along without a care in the world, and then suddenly—wham! We see a suggestive picture or someone walks by provocatively, and it seems that Satan is right there to whisper, "Hey, take a second look. Just looking won't do any harm. You aren't really sinning." Satan really is out to get us. He prowls around just looking for people to devour, and he is good at intimidation. He looks too strong to fight, and makes us feel that we are outnumbered, outclassed, and outsized.

The good news is that we are not powerless before his attacks. Satan may be bigger than we are, but he is not bigger than God is. God is our ally, and He has provided us with the armor and the weapons we need to win. Our problem is that we forget to use them. If we remember Who is for us, and resist the attacks of Satan, he will turn and run from us. We always have God on our side when we fight against sin, and Satan knows it. You do not have to be a superman or woman. You just have to say, "No!" and allow God's power to flow through your obedience to His commands.

Have you submitted your heart, soul, and mind to God? In what areas do you sometimes still struggle with saying "no" to temptation? To whom do you need to go for help?

_____

_____

_____

_____

_____

_____

_____

_____

DEVOTIONALS

DAY 9

Forgiveness

You do not delight in sacrifice, or I would bring it; you do not take pleasure in burnt offerings. The sacrifices of God are a broken spirit; a broken and contrite heart, O God, you will not despise (Psalm 51:16-17).

One of the sad results of sexual sin is the scars it leaves on those who engage in it. But, when a couple commits adultery, the two guilty parties are not the only ones affected. A marriage or maybe two may be broken apart. Innocent children will suffer. Parents and friends will grieve. Trust will be broken. Those who look up to the couple will be hurt.

When a person commits sexual sin, there is a heavy burden of guilt to bear. One sin leads to another, and the consequences reach farther than they would ever have imagined. Many times, they feel that God could never forgive them. They have gone too far, they are too guilty, they have harmed too many people. They can never, never make up for their sins. Nothing could ever pay for them.

Nothing, that is, but the blood of Christ. Jesus didn't die for the sin-free. He died for the guilty, for those who couldn't do anything to help themselves. He's not asking us to pay for our guilt. He did that. The only sacrifice God wants is repentance, a "broken and contrite heart."

Read all of Psalm 51. What do you need to confess to the Lord? Where do you need His healing touch?

_____

_____

_____

_____

_____

_____

_____

_____

_____

DEVOTIONALS

DAY 10

A Powerful Love

You did not put oil on my head, but she has poured perfume on my feet. Therefore, I tell you, her many sins have been forgiven—for she loved much. But he who has been forgiven little loves little. (Luke 7:46-47).

Jesus was eating in the home of a Pharisee, a high-ranking religious official. A woman came in and anointed His feet with perfume, which she brought in an alabaster jar. Luke describes her as "a woman who had lived a sinful life." She was probably a prostitute, or a woman who had committed adultery. The Pharisee was shocked that Jesus allowed such a woman to touch Him. He thought to himself that if Jesus were for real, He would have been able to tell who was touching Him. A righteous man would never knowingly let such a wicked woman come near him.

Jesus heard the Pharisee's thoughts, and turned to him with this story: Two men were in debt. One owed more than a year's wages. The other owed only a tenth of that sum. Neither had a penny, so the moneylender was moved with compassion and forgave their debts. Jesus asked which of the two would love the moneylender more?

A wretched sinner is not too much for God to forgive. Our past sins don't make us useless for future service in God's kingdom. Rather, the one who has been forgiven much loves much; he recognizes the mercy that God has shown him. That's when he is ready to show mercy to others. No matter how big your sins are, you can come with a repentant heart to God. He is willing and able to forgive and to make you clean and fit to serve Him.

How can you apply this story to your life? Where do you need forgiveness? Whom do you need to forgive?

_____

_____

_____

_____

_____

_____

_____

Avoid the Lure of Lust

1 Corinthians 6:18-20; James 1:12-15; 2 Timothy 2:22

If we really want to catch fish, we need to do two things. First, we find out what the fish eats. Second, we find out what turns the fish on—what gets it excited. And then we prepare the lure or bait so that it appeals to that particular fish.

Satan is a lot like a fisherman, but he is not out to get fish—he is after people. He finds out what turns us on and prepares bait to lure us into sin. One of these lures is the lure of lust. Lust is a unique sin because it has the most gender differences. For men, it tends to be obvious and overt. For women, it's often more subtle.

START IT UP

Our lives are filled with many more lures than just lust. Advertising is designed to lure us into buying more stuff, eating more food, or trying a new "miracle diet."

1. Do you think you are more likely to succumb to a food ad or a "stuff" ad? Why?

2. What is an example of an alluring advertisement someone might find tempting?

TALK IT UP

God's Word talks a lot about the temptation of lust. Let's face it; lust looms large in our world. Lust is "in." From advertising, to movies, lingering looks at the cute

guy in the office, a new romance novel to devour, the magazine rack with the latest swimsuit issue, or the Internet's images to download ... lust has a powerful lure!

Lust is fascinating because it uses our sexuality, yet it does not satisfy us sexually. Do you ever wonder why the sport of fishing keeps working, month after month, year after year? It seems that fish would eventually get the idea, "You know, every time one of my buddies strikes a lure, I never see him again. So, I'm not going near those things!" Sadly just like fish, we are caught every day by the lure of lust.

Learn to Recognize the Lure

Satan gets to us in gradual stages. *The first stage is casting the lure.* He's not in a hurry. He has been doing this for thousands of years. He just casts. He watches the spiritual depth finder in our lives. Satan can't read our minds, but he can read our responses. He watches what we do and say, who we spend time with, and what matters to us. He guesses when we're vulnerable or feeling invincible, and he tries to figure out what attracts us. Some of his lures we don't even notice—they don't appeal to us. Some get us so quickly that we don't even know what's happening.

The second stage is working the lure. Satan gives it a little splash, a little innuendo. He tries to bring our attention to pictures and words that start the imagination rolling. "What would it be like if ..." We begin to follow the bait and sin begins.

The third stage is the strike. When a fish first takes the bait, it doesn't realize it is hooked, and swims off. Then the fisherman sets the hook, and suddenly the fish is in trouble. A lot of us take the lure of lust and don't think anything is wrong. One day, Satan sets the hook and we are in trouble. You see, the sin is not in the lure, or in the bait. The sin is in the bite.

That brings us to the fourth stage—the fight. We splash and thrash, we ruin a marriage or two, and we mess up our children's lives. We throw a career aside just because of this simple lure of lust. And after Satan catches us, he doesn't throw us back. He takes us and mounts us on the wall ... a trophy of his victory!

Satan is our enemy, the one throwing out lures of lust, but we we can't blame it all on him. We can't just say, "I couldn't help it. The devil made me do it." James 1:14 points out that our temptations come right out ot the evil desires of our own hearts. How do we resist the lure of lust? The forces are strong, and we need to develop a plan, or it is just a matter of time before we will be mounted on Satan's wall.

Avoiding the Lure

Read 1 Corinthians 6:18-20

The Bible gives us one good tip for handling sexual temptation—"Flee from sexual immorality" (verse 18). In other words, "Run for your life!" We can't stick around thinking that we can handle this adversary, because we will always lose. Sexual temptation appeals to some of the strongest emotions and passions we have.

3. What could be some of the consequences in your life if you latch on to the lure of lust?

4. In what way is sexual immorality in particular a sin against one's own body?

5. What difference does it make that the Holy Spirit lives in us? What does it look like to honor God with one's body?

Safeguard: Battling Lust Before the Bait Drops

Starting to battle lust after it has grabbed us is just a little too late. We can pass by the lure, but getting away from full-fledged lust is much harder. The following "lust-busters" will help us skip the bait, so we can avoid taking the first bite.

Lust-buster #1—Refrain from flirtatious comments and gestures.
Lust-buster #2—Look past the lure of lust to the consequences.
Lust-buster #3—Monitor your media intake.
Lust-buster #4—Maximize your sexual relationship within your marriage.
Lust-buster #5—Establish accountability in your life.

6. Select one of these lust-busters and describe some practical ways to live it out in your life.

Read James 1:12-15

According to James, we can't enjoy lustful thoughts and expect it to end there. "Then, after desire has conceived," (that is, as soon as we entertain it for even just a few minutes), "it gives birth to sin."

7. This verse says that when sin is "full-grown," it gives birth to death. In what way does lust lead to death?

Safeguard: Don't Be a Lure Yourself

So far, we've been looking at this from one viewpoint: "How do I avoid lust?" We also need to look at it the other way around. Is there a chance that we are acting, speaking, or dressing in such a way that we are causing someone else to stumble?

This is how the gender differences in this sin really show up. Men and women have different lures, different triggers that lead them into wrong thoughts. As with so many human problems, we each assume that someone else's problems are the same as our own. We fail to be sensitive to the stumbling blocks of others.

This is not to say that it is all one-sided. Each of us is responsible for our own thought life, no matter what others do or wear or look like. But as Christ-followers, we also need to be aware of the needs of others, making sure that we are not the cause of another person's sin.

8. The lures of lust are different for men and women. What do men and women need to be aware of in order to be sensitive to the weaknesses of the opposite sex?

Fish in the Right Pond

Read 2 Timothy 2:22

Our first response to lust is to "flee." But putting off the old is never enough. We must put on the new. Besides running from lust—we must run after righteousness. When we're in hot pursuit of God, there's no room for the sidetrack of lust.

9. What does pursuing righteousness look like?

Have you ever said, "I wish temptation would just go away!"? Well, James 1:12 claims that temptation can actually be good for us. "Blessed is the man who perseveres under trial." Temptation is like a bench press, giving us opportunities to lift spiritual weights. Every time we say "no" to lust and flee from sin, we will be a little stronger and a little more able to resist. Even though we will never be free from temptation on this earth, we will be better able to handle it. And when serious temptation hits, we'll have strength to stand.

This is absolutely *not* to say that we should seek temptation. Jesus taught His disciples to pray "lead us not into temptation." The point is this: don't get mad at God for letting temptations come your way. Use the opportunity to grow stronger.

LIFT IT UP

Jesus showed a lot of compassion for people involved in sexual sin, including the woman at the well and the woman caught in adultery. Jesus essentially said, "I give you My grace, My forgiveness, My new life. Now, go and sin no more." No matter what you've done or where you've been, if you confess your sins and

repent, you can be made clean. God will forgive you and let you start over again.

Start now by saying to God, "I have made a covenant and commitment in my mind and heart to follow Your way for my sexual life and thoughts." He will give you the power, energy, and strength to walk on by—to resist the lure of lust. So, let's become the smart fish, the ones who see the lure of lust and just let it go floating by. With God's help, let's swim in the opposite direction. God wants us to be trophies for His kingdom, not stuffed and pinned to the wall of Satan's den.

10. Do you have collateral damage in your life from the lures of lust? How can this group pray for healing and restoration for you or your family?

11. How can this group help one another to be accountable in this area?

Take time to pray specifically for each other in those areas where strength, healing, or forgiveness is needed.

My Prayer Needs:

_____

_____

_____

_____

My Group's Prayer Needs:

_____

_____

_____

_____

_____

_____

_____

DEVOTIONALS

DAY 1

Flavorful Oblivion

When you sit to dine with a ruler, note well what is before you, and put a knife to your throat if you are given to gluttony (Proverbs 23:1-2).

Gluttony is essentially eating and drinking in excess. The word usually has a connotation of wastefulness and greed. We are all familiar with the idea that it is not good to be too overweight. Excess fat is bad for the health, and it can indicate some wrong emphasis on food. It is important for us to note, however, that the subject of gluttony is not just about comparing weight charts. Gluttony goes deeper than that. It is not just a sin of the body—it is a sin of the heart. A slender, fit person can have a heart attitude of gluttony just the same as an obese person can.

This proverb provides us with a vivid picture of the seriousness of gluttony. Imagine that a wealthy, influential leader has invited you for a meal. If you have habits of excess, you will make trouble for yourself. When you see the food, your thoughts will focus on it. You will be oblivious to anything but eating and drinking. If you are walking into deception, you will never know. If you are missing an amazing opportunity, it will pass you by. This proverb points out that giving in to gluttony is like cutting your own throat.

In what areas do you tend to be guilty of excess? What small step can you take today to gain some control?

_____

_____

_____

_____

_____

_____

_____

_____

_____

_____

DEVOTIONALS

DAY 2

A Wisdom-sized Appetite

Listen, my son, and be wise, and keep your heart on the right path. Do not join those who drink too much wine or gorge themselves on meat, for drunkards and gluttons become poor, and drowsiness clothes them in rags (Proverbs 23:19-21).

Avoiding gluttony is part of wisdom and simple common sense. Gluttony is a faulty focus on food. When the focus turns to food, we are going to lose in other ways. The most obvious loss is our health because gluttony abuses our bodies. When we eat and drink in excess, it dulls our senses and we become lethargic. Our bodies can't handle the poor food management. If the body is overwhelmed, the excess food is simply wasted, and we derive no nutritional benefit from it. Extra food is stored as excess fat, which brings in a whole new set of problems. But we can also be slender, weight-conscious gluttons. We may exercise and limit our portions so we don't put on the pounds, but our gluttony replaces good food with poor food. We starve our bodies of the nutrients they need, while dumping in an excess of junk food. Either way, we need to see that gluttony is not just another lifestyle choice—it is actually destructive.

How do you manage your diet? Are you keeping a sensible balance, or are you eating and drinking whatever you happen to crave?

_____

_____

_____

_____

_____

_____

_____

_____

_____

_____

_____

DEVOTIONALS

DAY 3

The Fruit We Don't Like

As Paul discoursed on righteousness, self-control and the judgment to come, Felix was afraid and said, "That's enough for now! You may leave. When I find it convenient, I will send for you" (Acts 24:25).

One of the strong roots of gluttony is lack of self-control. Self-control is a fruit of the Spirit that we do not usually like to talk about much. We like the idea of love, joy, peace, and kindness, but self-control is a different story. Self-control takes work and change. We are too much like Felix. The idea of self-control scares us. However, we have to remember that Paul was telling Felix the good news of the gospel. "Righteousness, self-control and the judgment" are part of it, but not all of it. Felix apparently missed the rest of the story. God did not leave us to live up to His standards by ourselves so we can escape judgment. He changes us and works in our lives so that we will be able to be like Him. It's overwhelming to think of having to do it all ourselves. But we're not on our own. The Holy Spirit came to help us so we can experience the fruit of self-control.

Are you scared of the idea of self-control? What is it that you don't want to give up? Ask the Holy Spirit to fill your life with His fruit (Galatians 5:22-23).

DEVOTIONALS

DAY 4

Self-control

You must teach what is in accord with sound doctrine. Teach the older men to be temperate, worthy of respect, self-controlled .... Likewise, teach the older women to be reverent in the way they live .... Then they can train the younger women ... to be self-controlled and pure .... Similarly, encourage the young men to be self-controlled. In everything set them an example by doing what is good (Titus 2:1-7).

Paul wrote this letter to his friend Titus, who was working with the church on the island of Crete. The Cretan culture had some problems. One of their own prophets said, "Cretans are always liars, evil brutes, lazy gluttons," and Paul and Titus both realized that this was often true. In fact, people in our culture also have these same problems, which result from a basic lack of self-control. Paul wanted Titus to emphasize this problem in his teachings. Older men, younger men, older women, younger women—there is no age or gender that is immune.

Today, the word "self-control" is almost bad language to some of us. We are taught that people need to be "free," that we should never suppress emotions, and that we deserve what we want. "Go ahead," we hear, "eat all the chocolate you want! Indulge yourself. Let your emotions hang out." "Be yourself" has come to mean, "Don't control yourself." We confuse self-control with stifled self-expression. It is true that we need to be able to express ourselves, and that it is okay to eat and do things we enjoy, but we have to ask the question: "Who or what is controlling my life?"

Are you in control of your emotions and desires, or do they control you? Take some time to pray and ask for God's help to identify and focus on those areas where your desires are controlling you.

_____

_____

_____

_____

_____

_____

_____

_____

DAY 5

Beating the Air?

Everyone who competes in the games goes into strict training. They do it to get a crown that will not last; but we do it to get a crown that will last forever. Therefore I do not run like a man running aimlessly; I do not fight like a man beating the air. No, I beat my body and make it my slave so that after I have preached to others, I myself will not be disqualified for the prize (1 Corinthians 9:25-27).

When we see great athletes, no one says, "Wow, that person was lucky to be born knowing how to do that. Isn't that interesting?" No, we all know that behind the brilliant performance are hours and hours of practice and hard work. Being excellent at something requires discipline. It requires self-control. A self-controlled person is not just uptight about life. This person is looking ahead, asking, "If I want to reach the goal and gain the prize, what do I need to do now? Is this something that will help me or hinder me? Do I really need it?"

In today's Scripture passage, Paul compares physical training with spiritual training. Body, emotions, and spirit are bound together so closely that we sometimes cannot tell where one ends and the other begins. As a result, what we do with our bodies does affect our spiritual life, just as our spiritual life and emotional life can affect our physical health.

Are you exercising discipline over your physical body as well as over your spiritual life, your thoughts, and emotions? What "training tips" from Paul can you begin to incorporate into your "fitness routine" this week?

_____

_____

_____

_____

_____

_____

_____

_____

DEVOTIONALS

DAY 6

Saying No

For the grace of God that brings salvation has appeared to all men. It teaches us to say "No" to ungodliness and worldly passions, and to live self-controlled, upright and godly lives in this present age (Titus 2:11-12).

The task of taking control of ourselves can look hopeless. We look at the mess we have made of our lives, and we don't even know where to start. We try to discipline ourselves, but in a few days we are back to our old ways. Why is this? What can we do?

The truth is we are not strong enough to take charge of our own lives. We try and try, and then we get tired and slip up again. We don't even always know when we should say "No." We need help, and God has given us the help we need. We don't have to try and earn it. God is ready to teach us when to say "No" to damaging things and to help us say "Yes" to the right things.

Read on in Titus 2:13-14. What is your motivation for being self-controlled? How can God's grace help you and teach you?

_____

_____

_____

_____

_____

_____

_____

_____

_____

_____

_____

_____

_____

_____

_____

DEVOTIONALS

DAY 7

Never Too Much

But the fruit of the Spirit is love, joy, peace, patience, kindness, goodness, faithfulness, gentleness and self-control. Against such things there is no law (Galatians 5:22-23).

Gluttony is a sin of excess. It takes something good and makes it into something bad by desiring and grasping for too much. The saying, "Moderation in all things" is a good rule of thumb to live by, except in one area— the fruit of the Spirit. When we have the Holy Spirit of God living inside us, we change. He produces in us a different kind of fruit—different actions and attitudes. Paul lists these new characteristics, and then says, "Against such things there is no law." In other words, you can never have too much love, joy, peace, patience, kindness, goodness, faithfulness, gentleness, and self-control. These virtues won't go bad with overuse, and we won't get sick if we take too much. There is always room for more.

What fruit of the Spirit are you seeing in your life now? What fruit do you need to cultivate and water?

_____

_____

_____

_____

_____

_____

_____

_____

_____

_____

_____

_____

_____

_____

DEVOTIONALS

DAY 8

Tipsy Turvy

Do not get drunk on wine, which leads to debauchery. Instead, be filled with the Spirit (Ephesians 5:18).

One of the forms of excess that is often a companion to gluttony is drunkenness. Overindulging in alcoholic beverages is a familiar problem. Many Christians have dealt with this by eliminating all alcohol from their diets. This way, the temptation to overindulge never comes up. This is a perfectly legitimate way to handle the threat of alcoholism, and a really good one if a person has a family history with this problem, or has come out of a lifestyle where this was an issue. It is a foolproof way to flee temptation and say "No" to ungodliness. While Christian leaders differ on whether alcohol is permissible or prudent for Christ-followers, there is no doubt about the trap of drunkenness.

Unlike most other foods, even a little excess of alcoholic beverages has a profound effect on our emotions, inhibitions, and reasoning ability. This euphoric quality is exactly the attraction to overindulgence. People like the feeling of well-being that alcohol brings, along with the temporary relief from trouble and heartache. Alcohol ends up being used as a poor substitute for the real comfort that comes from God. Alcohol, however, is not the only culprit. You might turn to fantasy, entertainment, food, clothes, technology, or some other counterfeit that you use to make yourself feel good instead of turning to God.

Where does your comfort come from? What do you find yourself relying on for comfort? What would help you learn to rely more on God for comfort?

_____

_____

_____

_____

_____

_____

_____

DAY 9

Taste Tester

Taste and see that the LORD is good; blessed is the man who takes refuge in him (Psalm 34:8).

Enjoying food is not a sin. God made food flavorful for our pleasure. However, it is sin to let pleasure in food lead one into excess, or to let it take God's place in our lives.

When we turn from our fixation on food, we need something to replace it. We have tasted and seen that ice cream is good. Chocolate makes us happy, and wine makes us mellow—large quantities of this or that will fill those holes we feel in our emotional well-being. If we give these things up, what will we have left? How can we cope with life if the refrigerator is not always there for us?

Try another flavor. Do a taste test. Invest the time and energy you used to give to food in a relationship with God. You will not be disappointed.

How can you invest more time and energy in your relationship with God today?

_____

_____

_____

_____

_____

_____

_____

_____

_____

_____

_____

_____

_____

_____

DEVOTIONALS

DAY 10

Got Satisfaction?

And I—in righteousness I will see your face; when I awake, I will be satisfied with seeing your likeness (Psalm 17:15).

We all go around looking for satisfaction in life. We want to be happy, we want to be successful, and we want to feel fulfilled. But there is only one place we will find that satisfaction. No material things are big enough. Even the best personal relationships cannot fill in all the gaps. Only when we find our satisfaction in God will we be free to experience joy. When we feel secure in who God is and who we are to Him, we will have firm ground to stand on. From this firm ground we can enjoy life, find beauty and pleasure in good things, love and be loved by other people ... without the desperate clutching we feel when we depend on these things for happiness and security.

Read Psalm 103:1-5 and 107:9. According to these verses, what "good things" does God long to give you? Focus this week on seeking out these good things.

_____

_____

_____

_____

_____

_____

_____

_____

_____

_____

_____

_____

_____

_____

Feast on the Good Stuff

Philippians 3:18-19; 1 Corinthians 3:16-17; 6:12-13,19-20; Proverbs 20:1; 23:1-3; 30:21-22; John 6:25-51

We live in a weight-oriented culture. An estimated one third of adults are over-weight. We're bombarded daily with ads promising to satisfy us with junk food. We are urged to indulge, to pamper ourselves, and to have a whole bag of whatever we want. At the next turn, a slender, sophisticated model is urging us to lose weight, to get fit, and to become beautiful. Her miracle diet will help us shed the pounds, while we eat all the junk we crave. We can lose the bulge and still indulge.

Our culture has a problem with gluttony. Now, some of you might be thinking, "Great, here is another study on how God only loves thin people. I don't even want to think about those extra pounds any more." On the other hand, some of you might be thinking, "Well, this week's session doesn't apply to me. I'm not overweight!" Before you tune out or get too smug, let's take a closer look at the subject of gluttony.

START IT UP

The subject of gluttony naturally brings up the subject of food. We all like to eat, and this is not bad. God made food tasty so that we would be able to derive pleasure from eating.

1. As a child, were you a picky eater? What foods did you truly like or dislike?

2. What is one of your favorite foods now?

TALK IT UP

If we are going to understand the sin of gluttony, we need to have a working definition of what it is. Webster's dictionary says that a glutton is "one who eats too much." Essentially, gluttony is lack of self-control, particularly as related to food. It is taking into our body more than it needs. The object of its affection is anything that is too much, too expensive, or too eagerly eaten. In other words, it is a faulty focus on food. A person's weight is not necessarily the best indicator of gluttony. Gluttony is not an issue of fit versus fat. It is a hint about the state of the heart. A "perfect physical specimen" could be just as guilty of gluttony as the person who is carrying around 50 extra pounds.

Gluttony Actually Is Sin

Read Philippians 3:18-19

Gluttony can be a really hard sin to identify. God made us so that we have to eat every day, and He also made food to be enjoyable. He could have given us flavorless fuel pellets to swallow every 12 hours, but instead He made us with taste buds, a sense of smell, and the capacity to enjoy food. Good food is one of God's good gifts. But just as it is with the other good things God has given us, our sinful flesh makes us capable of turning this good thing into a really bad thing.

In God's Word, two main types of excess are mentioned—food and alcohol.

"A fool who is full of food" (Proverbs 30:21-22) is a person who brings trouble to the world. Proverbs also warns against excess in drinking: "Wine is a mocker and beer a brawler; whoever is led astray by them is not wise" (Proverbs 20:1).

To the glutton, food or drink takes a priority that it was never meant to have in the human life. It begins to fill the thoughts, to direct the actions, and to provide security. It begins to take the place of God.

3. In what way could gluttony make one live as an enemy of Christ?

The Body Matters to God

Read 1 Corinthians 3:16-17 and 6:12-13,19-20

We know that the body is going to die. We are not going to live on this earth forever. We know that God is more interested in who we are than in how we look. He looks at the heart, while humans are busy worrying about the outside appearance. Knowing this, it is easy to assume that the body doesn't matter. Only spiritual things matter, so what you do with your body doesn't count. Actually, nothing could be further from the truth. Our physical bodies matter to God. First, our bodies are actually God's temple. When a person becomes a Christ-follower, God's Holy Spirit actually moves inside that person. When we abuse our physical bodies, we are abusing the place that God has chosen to live. Second, the way we handle our physical appetites affects our spiritual life. The link between the spiritual and the physical is very strong in human beings. Anything that we do with our physical bodies is going to have an effect on our spirits.

When we are talking about the natural appetite for food, we often think that this is one area that has nothing to do with God. Why would He care how much ice cream we eat? Surely spirituality isn't measured by grams of fat or milligrams of sodium intake.

God hasn't given us a list of rules and a "holy calorie count." Instead, He has given us freedom. *The key here is who our master is. Our stomachs and our pleasures in food and drink are not going to last forever.* They are going to come to an end, like other earthly things. What is driving us? What is running our lives? Is it God, or is it physical appetites?

4. Who controls your life: God or your physical appetites? How can you tell?

5. What might "honoring God with your body" look like in the area of food?

Self-Control and Trust

Read Proverbs 23:1-3

One of the big underlying issues connected with the sin of gluttony is lack of self-control. We have already identified gluttony as eating in excess of the body's needs. It is really easy to point a finger at the 400-pounders, but we have to realize that a person without an excess ounce can have an attitude of gluttony that is just as bad in God's sight. This is the attitude of self-indulgence, the attitude that says, "I'll eat as much of this as I want, I don't care whether it is good for me or not, whether it is too expensive or not, whether I need it or not." A person could never exceed 1600 calories a day, but most of those calories could come from gorging on ice cream. Just because someone's waistline doesn't advertise it for them, they still may be dealing with self-indulgence and gluttony. We may wonder why this should be a problem. After all, as long as we're not overweight, why should anyone care what we actually eat? The answer is found in the fact that what we do with our body affects our spirit. If we cannot say "no" about something as simple and small as food, how will we be able to say "no" to the bigger temptations? Self-indulgence makes us spiritually soft.

The second underlying cause of gluttony is often lack of trust in God. Instead of turning to God, we use food as a means of comfort, as a way of feeling in control of our lives. Food really can give an emotional lift. It gives a sensation of suddenly and instantaneously feeling better. We can have a disagreement with our spouse. We can have a stress-filled day at the office. We can experience the breakup of a dating relationship. But we can always, always show a half-gallon of ice cream who is boss. The refrigerator won't yell back at us. Many of us turn food into an emotional bandage to cover a gaping wound that we have suffered. At that time, food becomes our god. We try to let food soothe our wounds. But "food is deceptive," as our passage in Proverbs tell us. It is only a quick fix; it is a counterfeit of God's love, grace, and forgiveness.

6. In what ways could an attitude of gluttony affect other areas of your life?

7. How are a lack of self-control and a lack of trust in God contributing to the sin of gluttony in your life?

109

Feast on the Real Bread of Life

As always, there is no point in gaining control of gluttony if we don't replace it with something else. Many people who are sincerely trying to avoid gluttony become so obsessed with fitness and health food that those become a different form of idolatry. We may be able to avoid gluttony, but unless we change our focus from food to God, we will be no better off than before. We will begin to derive security from our exercise programs, fresh carrot juice, organic produce, and whole-grain bread. Food will still be our god. It is important to be good stewards of our bodies, but the focus can't be on the house. It has to be on the One who lives in the house.

Read John 6:25-51

You may already be familiar with the story of Jesus miraculously feeding the 5,000 with only two fish and five small loaves of bread. A huge crowd had been following Him and listening to His teaching and Jesus felt compassion for their physical hunger as well as their spiritual hunger. He gave them a satisfying meal of real physical food, and the people were very impressed. They followed Him, thinking that they would never have to find food again if Jesus would continue to do such miracles. But Jesus pointed them in a different direction.

God made us with desires, but they've become warped. Food isn't worth focusing on. This isn't a question of fat versus fit or junk food versus health food. It is a question of where our focus is. Only Jesus can really satisfy, and really comfort us. Only God is worthy of being given the top priority in our lives.

8. How does Jesus contrast the manna (a gift from God) and Himself (also from God)? What does this tell us about the importance we should place on physical food?

9. What can we do when the pull of food feels too strong to resist?

LIFT IT UP

When you drive around a residential neighborhood, do you ever stop to wonder how many of the houses are actually the homes of families founded on Jesus Christ, structured with His love and powered by His Holy Spirit? God is definitely concerned with our bodies, but He is so much more intimately and vitally concerned with whether or not we create a home for His Holy Spirit. He wants His Holy Spirit to live and breathe and work in our lives and through our lives. Most of us will never bear the title Mr. or Ms. Universe. But every single one of us has the potential to carry a much more significant title—Temple of the Holy God.

10. What place do you think food really plays in your life?

11. What will you do in the coming week to make some "home improvements" for God's temple?

Take time to pray specifically for each other in those areas where your desires and priorities need to be restructured.

My Prayer Needs:

_____

_____

_____

_____

My Group's Prayer Needs:

_____

_____

_____

_____

_____

_____

_____

_____

DAY 1

The Stuff Sprouts Wings

Do not wear yourself out to get rich; have the wisdom to show restraint. Cast but a glance at riches, and they are gone, for they will surely sprout wings and fly off to the sky like an eagle (Proverbs 23:4-5).

Greed is a basic human problem. People deal with greed no matter what their situation in life is. It doesn't matter how much we have—we can always want more. In our culture, we have access to so much that it is easy to gratify greed. We can accumulate with minimal cost and effort. It is so simple that we don't even recognize our greed. Even though accumulation is easy and doesn't seem to hurt anyone, God's Word tells us that it is wise to show restraint. When we get the "I wants," we need to think ahead a little. Are we depending too much on these things? Because these things just will not last. We think our possessions are permanent, but it takes only one little disaster for everything to be gone. A fire, a hurricane, a business failure, a theft—these can all sweep away our material things before our very eyes.

When deciding to make a purchase, how often do you ask yourself, "Do I really need this? Am I putting too much energy into getting something that won't last?" What material things do you wish you had not purchased, and why?

_____

_____

_____

_____

_____

_____

_____

_____

_____

_____

_____

_____

DEVOTIONALS

DAY 2

Never Enough

Whoever loves money never has money enough; whoever loves wealth is never satisfied with his income. This too is meaningless. As goods increase, so do those who consume them. And what benefit are they to the owner except to feast his eyes on them? The sleep of a laborer is sweet, whether he eats little or much, but the abundance of a rich man permits him no sleep (Ecclesiastes 5:10-12).

The grip of greed continually tightens on our lives. At first, we only want a little more. We think, "If only I had enough money to be able to afford this one little thing, I would be happy." We only want to be able to travel more often, or have a car with a few "extras," or be able to get a little bit nicer coat. So we strive to get this one thing, and then once we have it, it doesn't satisfy the way we thought it would. We want more. We think of another new thing that we just cannot live without.

It always works this way. The more we get, the more we want. Greed brings us to the point where we don't even enjoy what we have anymore. What's the point of 50 pairs of shoes when we only have two feet? What's the point of a few extra millions when we already own everything we have ever wanted? Greed will bring us to a point of even greater dissatisfaction. We will be sitting in the midst of our possessions, knowing we are not at peace, and we can't even think of something else to want. There will be nothing left to work for.

Are you feeling dissatisfied with your life? What are you pursuing to make you happier? Do you think it will succeed?

DAY 3

You Can't Take It with You

Naked a man comes from his mother's womb, and as he comes, so he departs. He takes nothing from his labor that he can carry in his hand (Ecclesiastes 5:15).

When we grasp the concept of death, we are going to understand why gratifying greed is so futile. When we die, we take nothing with us. All we have owned and earned will stay right here on earth for our descendants to fight over. All the energy we put into accumulating material goods is a waste, as far as we are concerned. We come into the world with no assets but a body, and when we depart this world, we don't even have that. It's a sobering thought. But thinking about death can give us a good perspective on life.

What are some things you are putting your efforts and money into that don't really matter? What are some of your eternal investments?

_____

_____

_____

_____

_____

_____

_____

_____

_____

_____

_____

_____

_____

_____

_____

DEVOTIONALS

DAY 4

Treasure Trove

Do not store up for yourselves treasures on earth, where moth and rust destroy, and where thieves break in and steal. But store up for yourselves treasures in heaven, where moth and rust do not destroy, and where thieves do not break in and steal. For where your treasure is, there your heart will be also (Matthew 6:19-21).

So often, humans are like crows. We grab at anything that glitters, without a thought for its real value. The treasures we choose are perishable. They can go bad, they can be stolen, and they can be destroyed in a storm, a fire, or a financial disaster. God's Word tells us to choose a different kind of treasure and a different bank. When we put our efforts into making money and accumulating stuff, we accumulate a treasure we can see and touch. When we put our efforts into loving God and serving others, it is like putting money in the bank of heaven. It will last, and it will be waiting for us when we get there. This is not a matter of storing up good deeds for salvation, but God does say that in the end He will judge and reward us according to what we do now.

When you come before Christ at the last day, what will your "heavenly bank account" have in it? Will He look at you and say, "Well done!" or will you hang your head in shame? Read 1 Corinthians 3:10-15.

_____

_____

_____

_____

_____

_____

_____

_____

_____

_____

_____

_____

DAY 5

Who Is Your Boss?

No one can serve two masters. Either he will hate the one and love the other, or he will be devoted to the one and despise the other. You cannot serve both God and Money (Matthew 6:24).

We have only a limited amount of energy, time, and devotion. It's enough to live on, but it's not enough to divide. We cannot choose more than one real priority, more than one lifestyle. We cannot serve more than one master. Sometimes we think that we can do both at once—we can work for money during the week and then serve God on the weekends. Sometimes we think we can take turns. "I'll get established first," we say, "Then I'll retire early, and I'll be able to use all the money I earned for ministry."

Our hearts have room for only one throne. We only have devotion enough for one master. We can only focus on one goal at a time. If we choose the goal of money, we won't keep our love for God. This won't happen all at once, but bit by bit, we will push Him out of our lives. We won't want Him distracting us from our pursuit of cash. We won't want Him reminding us of those who need things more than we do. We will stop talking to Him because we don't want to hear that we should change our focus. We will stop reading His Word because we won't want to come across verses like Matthew 6:24.

Looking at your schedule and activities for this past week, who would you say is your master? What are your priorities at this time in your life?

_____

_____

_____

_____

_____

_____

_____

_____

_____

_____

DEVOTIONALS

DAY 6

Root of Evil

People who want to get rich fall into temptation and a trap and into many foolish and harmful desires that plunge men into ruin and destruction. For the love of money is a root of all kinds of evil. Some people, eager for money, have wandered from the faith and pierced themselves with many griefs (1 Timothy 6:9-10).

Paul's first letter to Timothy ends with a serious warning about the love of money. "Men of corrupt mind," Paul wrote, "have been robbed of the truth and ... think that godliness is a means to financial gain" (1 Timothy 6:5). This "Prosperity Gospel" is a popular version of God's plan for us. God loves us; therefore, God will make us rich. If we are not rich, it is because we are in sin or lacking in faith. If we please God, the cash will come across. This is the classic appeal to basic greed. We have to be good so that our spiritual Santa Claus will bring us more presents.

There is not necessarily anything wrong with being rich. But, the desire to be rich is not godly—it is dangerous. God's Word reminds us repeatedly that money and material possessions will not last. They are only on earth, and even here, they cannot be trusted. Our security has to come from something else.

If we want to build our lives on something that can be trusted, then we will build it on faith in God. We can trust Him to provide for our needs and keep us out of the treasure traps.

What kinds of "traps" have you seen people fall into because of the love of money? When have you encountered some of these" traps" in your life? What were the consequences?

_____

_____

_____

_____

_____

_____

_____

_____

DAY 7

A New Pursuit

But you, man of God, flee from all this, and pursue righteousness, godliness, faith, love, endurance and gentleness (1 Timothy 6:11).

Greed is our enemy. It will lead us into both sin and grief. We have to run from it. But if we are going to be successful in conquering greed in our lives, we have to replace it with something better. All of the energy we have put into pursuing things we need to put into pursuing God. We expend an amazing drive, incredible creativity, endurance, patience, and intelligence on gaining wealth. The sad thing is that we are wasting the power of these God-given tools. If we turn that power to the pursuit of godliness, we are going to have some incredible results.

What resources and abilities do you use to gain wealth? How could you use these to pursue God?

DEVOTIONALS

DAY 8

Living Free

Keep your lives free from the love of money and be content with what you have, because God has said, "Never will I leave you; never will I forsake you." So we say with confidence, "The Lord is my helper; I will not be afraid. What can man do to me?" (Hebrews 13:5-6).

Love of money and pursuit of wealth are really a way of saying, "God, I don't really trust you. I think that if I want to be comfortable, I have to take care of myself. I don't really believe that heaven will be better than earth, so I have to get my pleasure now." Trusting in God turns greed into contentment. Contentment is not lethargy or lack of interest. It is an understanding of what really matters. Even if we don't have as much as we would like, we can say, "I know God is taking care of me. He promised He would. I'll trust Him to make good out of whatever He brings my way."

Are you content with what you have right now? What more do you want? What do you think your motives are for wanting this? If you don't get it, will it spoil your peace?

_____

_____

_____

_____

_____

_____

_____

_____

_____

_____

_____

_____

_____

DAY 9

Just Enough

Two things I ask of you, O LORD; do not refuse me before I die: Keep falsehood and lies far from me; give me neither poverty nor riches, but give me only my daily bread. Otherwise, I may have too much and disown you and say, "Who is the LORD?" Or I may become poor and steal, and so dishonor the name of my God (Proverbs 30:7-9).

Have you ever prayed for God to make you rich—or at least a little richer? We tend to think that financial prosperity is the ultimate sign of God's blessing, and even if we don't voice the thought, we would really like to try out being rich. But if our goal is really to honor God in everything we do, then we should be asking: "Please give me no more than I can handle. I don't want anything that would turn me away from You." It may sound strange to ask God to keep you from getting too rich, but it is a request that will keep us from certain sin. When we have more than we need, we stop depending on God. The Lord's Prayer says, "Give us this day our daily bread." How many of us really think about our daily food coming from God? When we think about our finances, our goal should not be "just a little more," it should be "just enough."

What are you doing with the "extra" that God has given you over and above your basic needs? How can you glorify God with your riches?

_____

_____

_____

_____

_____

_____

_____

_____

_____

_____

_____

_____

DEVOTIONALS

DAY 10

For the Rich

Command those who are rich in this present world not to be arrogant nor to put their hope in wealth, which is so uncertain, but to put their hope in God, who richly provides us with everything for our enjoyment. Command them to do good, to be rich in good deeds, and to be generous and willing to share. In this way they will lay up treasure for themselves as a firm foundation for the coming age, so that they may take hold of the life that is truly life (1 Timothy 6:17-19).

When God blesses us financially, it means He has given us special responsibilities:

First, we have to guard against arrogance. We cannot start thinking that we have so much because we are special. We have this because God has given it to us.

Second, we must make sure our hope is in the right place. Our wealth will not keep us safe or make us happy—it is only a tool God has given us for doing good.

Third, we should use our wealth to bless others by giving to those who have less than we do.

Many of us read these verses and think, "Well, that's not me. I'm not one of those with a six-figure income. I'm not rich." *Think again!* In comparison with the rest of the world, most of us are fabulously wealthy. We have food, clothing, shelter, security, and even extras like ice cream and pictures on our walls. We can stop looking around for the rich Christ-followers who should share their wealth. We are those rich people.

What are you doing to follow God's instructions for the wealthy? What can you do to be more generous with what God has given you?

_____

_____

_____

_____

_____

_____

Escape the Grip of Greed

**Proverbs 11:24-28; 2 Corinthians 9:1-15;
1 Corinthians 16:1-2; Luke 12:15**

When professional wrestlers are putting on their theatrical matches, there is always one hold or maneuver that knocks the other wrestler out cold. This is the "sleeper hold." One wrestler will come up behind the other one, put his giant arms around his opponent's head, and squeeze. Once the grip is on, the match is over. The referee will ring the bell, and the match will end. The same is true of the grip of greed.

Today we will conclude this series by discussing the seventh fatal distraction—greed. The Bible is full of examples of greed. Greed for knowledge and power caused Adam and Eve to take the forbidden fruit (Genesis 3:6-7). Greed caused Jacob to cheat his brother out of the blessing of the firstborn (Genesis 27:1-40). Greed caused the moneychangers to set up shop in the temple (Mark 11:15-19). Greed caused Judas to betray Jesus for 30 pieces of silver (Matthew 26:14-16). Greed ultimately cost the rich young man his eternity in heaven. (Mark 10:17-31). All these people were in the "sleeper hold" of greed, and they could not escape it.

START IT UP

Our culture has a fixation on the accumulation of more and more "stuff." We all have this tendency, and we all deal with it in different ways. Naturally, we each think our ways are the best.

1. Are you more likely to be a "saver" or a "pitcher"? Do you tend to keep junk "just in case it comes in handy someday" or do you throw everything away and go out and buy new stuff when you need it?

2.   Are you and your family on the same page with "saving" or "pitching"?

TALK IT UP

Greed can be defined as an insatiable desire to acquire. This fatal distraction bombards us everywhere we turn. Advertisers spend billions of dollars creating images, sights, and sounds that will infiltrate our brains and make their products seem so irresistible that we will become fixated on them and need to acquire them. The Bible calls greed a grievous sin. Greed is listed along with such nasty counterparts as murder, deceit, sexual immorality, idolatry, and drunkenness.

It is easy for us in today's culture to feed our greed. We live in the most prosperous civilization on earth, and more and more "stuff" is easy to come by. We can greedily acquire all this "stuff" without ever feeling greedy, because we don't have to struggle to gratify the greed. We can reach out and take whenever we feel the first twinge of "I want …"

What is God's read on greed? God says there is only one thing that will break the back of greed— generosity. We have to take off greed and put on generosity. Generosity will break the hold of greed because it is the antithesis of greed. Greed is selfish. Generosity is open-handed. Greed is keeping a list of things you want. Generosity is keeping a list of things you can do to help others.

In the ninth chapter of 2 Corinthians, Paul is encouraging the Corinthians to get out of their comfort zone and begin to be generous. We might wonder why Christians need encouragement to give. We ought to be the most generous people in the world. We serve a generous God who has given His grace to us in great abundance. Besides, we know that money won't last—we can't take it to heaven with us. But the truth is, we are still sinners, and even though we may know these things, we still struggle with greed.

Benefit #1: Blessings

Living a life of generosity has many benefits. The first benefit is that a life of generosity brings bountiful blessing. God's Word says that we will harvest

blessings in direct proportion to the way we plant generosity. Malachi 3:10 says that if we are generous, God will "throw open the floodgates of heaven and pour out so much blessing that you will not have room enough for it."

Read Proverbs 11:24-28

At first glance, it seems that this is an appeal to basic greediness. Give generously so that we can get more. Is that what God is saying to us? No. Many times, God does bless a generous person financially. However, generosity is not just a God-sanctioned method for getting rich. God blesses generous people financially, because generous people have proven that they can use their wealth in a God-pleasing way. All of life involves getting. The key is to know what kind of "getter" you are. Some of us are Velcro-getters. We get things and they stick to us. We walk around with things hanging all over us saying, "That's mine!" Don't be a Velcro-getter. Take the Velcro off and put on a Teflon outfit. Teflon-getters receive stuff and it just slides off them. They get so they can give.

3. What does hoarding say about our trust in God? How about generosity?

4. What would "Teflon-getting" look like in your life? Be specific and practical.

Benefit #2: Stirring up Others

Read 2 Corinthians 9:1-5

The second benefit of generosity is the way it can encourage others and stir "them to action" (verse 2). When one generous person goes into action, other people see the results and they are encouraged to follow that example. More and more people will look at what happens when you wear the Teflon suit, and they will want to get rid of their Velcro.

5. Read 1 Corinthians 16:1-2. What are the benefits of the method described here for implementing generosity? How might this make it easier to give generously, not grudgingly?

Benefit #3: Hilarious Generosity

Read 2 Corinthians 9:6-7

Have you ever met a negative, generous person? The two characteristics just do not go together. This illustrates the third benefit of generosity. When we give to someone in need, it opens up windows of opportunity for God to step into our lives and supernaturally intervene and bless us.

In verse seven, Paul tells us "God loves a cheerful giver." The Greek word translated "cheerful" is the root of our English word "hilarious." God is not looking for us to un-padlock our wallets once every pay period, take out exactly 10% to the penny, and then say, "Here God, you can have this. I really don't want to give it up, but this is the exact amount I owe you. Now don't bother me for any more." That is not generosity. That is an obligatory payment. God is looking for us to give cheerfully, joyfully, hilariously. Giving is not a chore—it's a privilege God has shared with us.

When we share the material blessings that God has given us with others, we form a special bond of love with the receiver. Have you ever received an unexpected gift from someone—particularly something that you needed? How did you feel? Giving to those in need says, "I care." When people feel cared about, they can turn around and give that same message to others.

6. What are some practical ways we can "sow generously"?

7. What can we do to change our attitudes and become cheerful, generous givers?

Wrestle Free From Greed

Read 2 Corinthians 9:8-15

A life of generosity will naturally grow in grace. When we put our money where our mouth is—when our walk and talk match—then others will praise God because of us.

> 8. According to these verses, what will the fruits of generosity look like? List some of the results of generous living.

Many people think that there is too much talk about money in church, so they shake their heads and turn off their minds and hearts when it's discussed. However, did you realize that the Bible is full of talk about money? Sixteen of Jesus' 38 parables had to do with money. Over and over the Bible talks about how people should handle their money and possessions. When we get to the judgment seat, God is going to ask us, "What did you do with the resources I gave you? Did you listen to what I said in My Word about handling those resources?" One day we will be held accountable for what we did with our material blessings, what we knew, and what we should have known.

Read Luke 12:15 for an important warning!

Greed is not an attitude that we consciously decide to adopt. It is something that creeps up behind us and grabs us around the neck, like the "sleeper hold." We have to be on guard, using four maneuvers to release the grip of greed.

Maneuver One

Learn to admire an object without having to own it. This ability will save us thousands and thousands of dollars. All of us have something in our lives that could easily become a fixation if we let it get out of focus. If we develop that insatiable desire to acquire, then we will fall right into greed. When that happens, our goods become our gods, and we have stepped over the line into greed. Think about it this way—if we don't own something, we don't have to insure it, maintain it, shine it, or watch it depreciate. We can look at it, admire it, and walk away. There is nothing wrong with admiring something beautiful. We are applauding the creative genius of God.

Maneuver Two

Learn the secret of giving stuff away. We have to learn to give away the items we are tightly holding onto. Every time we give, we are escaping the grip of greed. Go ahead—give away something that you think is really important to you. Give a gift that will give your bank account a coronary. You might find that it doesn't matter as much as you thought it did. You may find that you don't even notice it's gone.

Maneuver Three

Develop contentment. When the Bible talks about contentment, it is not talking about a lack of ambition or drive. The Bible never says that it is God's will for all Christians to be poor, to never excel in anything, or to settle for status quo. That is not the point. The point is what owns you? Money itself is neutral, like any other tool. It doesn't give off evil rays or contaminate anyone who looks at it. Money can accomplish good things. Money is necessary for the basics of life. But money can also be a tool that causes great harm. Either we have money, or money has us. We have to be able to use money without it owning us.

Contentment does not have to do with what we have or don't have; it's about who we are in Christ. When we know who we are in Christ, we can be content with a lot or a little, because we know that money is not what matters. We can take it or leave it. A contented person doesn't need to change his or her position in life in order to feel all right about him or herself. A contented person knows that security comes only from Christ, and the wealth or lack of it is a side issue. Things are great, but things do not bring lasting joy. Many wealthy people have bankrupt personal lives.

9. If you remained financially at the same level you are now for the rest of your life, would you be content? Would you be joyful? On what do you really base your happiness?

Maneuver Four

Recognize the reality of death. Death is the final failure of things. Nothing we accumulate means very much when we contemplate death. Think about how you want people to remember you. Do you want them to say things like, "Yeah, he had a huge pile of cash" and "She really knew how to keep the money rolling in"? Or do you want them to say things like, "He was so quick to help me when I was in need" and "She gave and gave, even though I know she was tired and didn't have much"? Think about how the Christians at Joppa remembered Dorcas, as they deeply grieved over her death. When Peter arrived they didn't show him her bank statement or her million-dollar lakeside residence. Instead the group of poor people gathered there said, "Look at what she gave me. Look at what she did for me when I was in need" (see Acts 9:36-39). If we want to escape the "sleeper hold" of greed, we should become generous in everything we do.

LIFT IT UP

Professional wrestling always has tag-team matches. One wrestler stands on the ring apron and extends his hand if the other wrestler is in trouble. All the other wrestler has to do is reach out and touch his partner's hand, and he then jumps over the ring ropes to save the day. Are you feeling that you are caught in the grip of greed and you can't get away? Do you feel like the referee is getting ready to ring the bell? There is great news for you. God is in your corner. God is on the ring apron. He is stretching out His arms to you and all you have to do is reach out and tag His hand. The moment you touch His hand, He will come in and deliver you from the grip of greed.

As we conclude this study on the seven fatal distractions, take a minute to think back over the things we have talked about over the last few weeks. Each one of these sins is something that every Christ-follower has to deal with at some level. No one is immune. Furthermore, every one of these sins is something that we need God's help to deal with. We cannot come clean by sweeping all the darkness out of our lives. We can only come clean by letting the light in—the light of Jesus Christ. We have to look at sin, understand what it is, and learn how to get rid of it. But we shouldn't focus on the sins—we will only increase our problems. It's a little like driving a car. Staying on our side of the yellow line is essential. However, we can't stay there by focusing on the ground just outside of the driver's side window. We focus on the road ahead and drive steadily toward our destination.

"... let us run with perseverance the race marked out for us. Let us fix our eyes on

Jesus, the author and perfecter of our faith, who for the joy set before him endured the cross, scorning its shame, and sat down at the right hand of the throne of God" (Hebrews 12:1b-2).

10. Where is your focus in life now? How does your relationship with Jesus Christ fit in with your goals and direction?

11. Which fatal distraction most threatens to lead you off-course? How can this group pray for you?

Take time to pray specifically for each other in those areas where you feel the Holy Spirit is calling you to "change your clothes" from sin to virtue.

My Prayer Needs:

_____

_____

_____

_____

My Group's Prayer Needs:

Donna   Kids starting schools

Leila   Ashley - Results of Bone Scan - Scott's Job

Megan - daughter - Results of tests (trouble breathing)

Brandon - back to school

Jeff - Nephew - moved to Las Vegas

Debbie - brother in Iraq

Todd + Barbara - Real Estate

- Children

All Troops - In Iraq

Whether you're a brand new small-group leader or a longtime veteran, this leader's guide is designed to help you make the most of your group time. It will help you facilitate a healthy discussion among the members of your group, as well as provide you with insight and answers to questions in each session. Remember to check here not only for answers to questions you are unsure about, but also for ideas on how to involve everyone, and how to bring creativity to the discussions.

Throughout this study there are a few places where you will encounter large sections of Scripture to read. As the leader, you should encourage members of your group to come to your meeting time prepared, having read the session, checked Scripture references, and answered the questions. That way you can summarize these large blocks rather than risk losing people's attention while someone reads aloud. But, be careful not to assume everyone knows these Bible stories, and make sure your summaries give the important points. Doing this will help you maintain a smooth flow in the discussion as you stay on target (and on time) in your group.

Leading a small group can be challenging, but it also brings many rewards, so invest some time in preparing yourself to lead. You'll be delighted with the results!

SESSION 1 – Off with the Old, On with the New

Objectives:
- To understand the change that happens when we become Christ-followers
- To learn how to "put on" new actions and attitudes that will reflect Christ in our lives and protect us from being distracted by sin

1. What did you work the hardest to learn when you were growing up? Sports? Music lessons? Academics? What did you find the most rewarding?

    Tip: Listen to the answers and follow up by asking why the members felt more rewarded by something. (Example: "Was it because you were naturally good at that, or because you had to work hard to succeed at it?")

2. Who was the hero or role model you most looked up to—someone who inspired you to really put your heart into what you were doing?

    Tip: As people answer this question take note of whether or not they actually knew this model or were inspired by someone "untouchable" like an actor/actress or sports hero. Point out that as we grow up in our Christian faith, we should be inspired by that real relationship with Jesus. He may not be physically visible, but He is certainly knowable!

3. What does the phrase "Christ, who is your life" (verse 4) mean? In what way is Christ your life?

    A: Jesus Christ is life for Christ-followers in that He has given us the power to live our lives for Him, right now, today. That means those who know Him, who choose to follow Him, have the power to be freed from the sinful patterns they formed in their lives before.

4. What are some examples of "things above" to set your mind on (verse 2)? How real do these things seem to you?

    A: These "things above" are what the Bible tells us have eternal value, such as communicating the gospel, loving one another, investing in the local church, honoring God, and serving His purposes. We must see the things that will be important in the future—when we live "above" in heaven.

5. Practically speaking, how can you "put to death" the behaviors that belong to the old nature? What can you do to break old patterns and habits? Be specific.

    A: It all starts with prayer. Ask God to reveal to you which of your habits are offensive to Him. This may mean completely changing some of your routines such as: where you go; who you spend time with; and what you read, watch, or listen to. Then, one very practical way to get rid of old rooutines is to replace them with new ones—something pleasing to God. (Encourage specific, real-life examples vs. general, theoretical responses.)

6. Pick out one of these sins and give a specific example of how it can destroy our potential to effectively follow Christ. (Pride; Anger; Envy; Slothfulness; Lust; Gluttony; Greed)

    A: Any/all of these sins can damage or even destroy our ability to effectively follow Christ. When we engage in these habits, we are focused on meeting our needs, following the ways of the world or our sinful desires, instead of trusting in Jesus. We take the role of god of our universe.

7. If you are comfortable, can you share a time when you thought you had swept your life clean of sin or a problem, only to have it come back later and even stronger?

    Tip: Be prepared to open this discussion with an example from your own life, but be careful about being deeply vulnerable.

8. Compare the list of virtues in Colossians 3:12-14 with the list of sins in verses 5-9. How do these virtues counteract the vices of the first list?

   Tip: Pick one or two to discuss in your time together. Do not go down the full list one by one, spending a lot of time on each.

9. What does it mean to "let the word of Christ dwell in you richly" (Colossians 3:16)? How can we do this, and what will it accomplish in our lives?

   A: This refers to learning and applying Scripture in our lives, individually and together as a group. Memorizing Scripture is a great aid. There are several ways to begin memorizing Scripture, so share some creative strategies.

10. How can we show love to one another in this group? Share practical ideas and prayer requests so that you can be healed and happy.

    Tip: As people answer, write down their ideas. As this discussion winds down, relate back what has been said. Then, challenge yourself and the rest of the group to start living out these ideas.

11. Do you have the Spirit of God at work in your life? If you are not sure, the leader of the group will be glad to talk to you and help you.

    Tip: Leader, always be prepared to share the plan of salvation with a member. A useful tool is a small, simple-to-read pamphlet called a "tract" that explains salvation. There are many varieties, and they are generally available at Christian bookstores. Pick some up, read them to become familiar, and prepare to guide someone through them when God gives you opportunity. Another effective tool is simply sharing your own faith story.

SESSION 2 – Get Off the Pride Ride

Objectives:
- To identify what pride looks like and how it poisons our relationships
- To discuss practical steps that will help us get off the "pride ride"

1. What fictional character (from a movie, TV show, or book) do you think of as a classic example of pride?

2. What characteristics does this fictional character have that really demonstrate this trait of pride?

   Tip: Leader, remember that the first question or two in each session is to get people talking and make the rest of your discussion flow easier. There's no right or wrong answers so relax, enjoy, and let the others do the same!

3. How can we tell the difference between a proper self-concept and self-conceit?

    A: A proper self-concept takes into consideration that the basis for a person's worth is their identity in Christ. When I see myself as God sees me—a sinner He loved enough to die for—I gain a proper self-concept, with a good balance of humility and confidence in Him. With self-conceit, I view myself as successful according to the world's standards. Self-conceit leads to self-dependence instead of God-dependence.

4. How do we, as humans, try to put ourselves in God's place?

    A: One way is by relying on ourselves—our wisdom, our strength, our good looks, etc.—to bring success or fulfillment. In this, we ignore God as our source of fulfillment and put ourselves in His rightful role. Another way is by living by our own rules, deciding we know better than God how to live life. Disobedience is evidence that we've put ourselves in God's place.

5. What impresses you most about Jesus washing the disciples' feet?

    Tip: Good follow-up questions are, "Why do you think He did it?" or "How do you think the disciples felt as Jesus humbly served them?" The point you ultimately want to land on is simply that Jesus washed their feet to demonstrate that to truly follow Him ... they had to put aside their pride.

6. What will look different in our lives if we are giving God the credit for our accomplishments?

    A: By staying off the pride ride and recognizing God as the One who works through us, we can maintain a healthy self-image, develop a deeper relationship with Him, and find real contentment. Instead of being overwhelmed by the pressure to perform, we can have confidence that God will enable us to do what needs to be done. With success, we will not be arrogant, because we recognize God as the source of anything we accomplish. If we "fail," we don't have to be devastated because we know that God's acceptance is not dependent on our performance.

7. Think about your primary relationships. What are some ways that pride has caused distance in these relationships?

    Tip: Leader, this question requires people to look hard at their lives. Some may answer superficially or be reluctant to share how their pride has pushed people away. Model transparency and vulnerability by sharing first.

8. What are some practical ways we can spend time daily worshipping God?

A: Worship is a 24-hour-a-day, 7-day-a-week activity. Everything should be done as an act of worship. That means approaching your daily routine as if everything you do is being done for God Himself! When you take out the trash, do it for God. When you change a diaper, do it for God. When you close a deal, do it for God. It's also key to develop an attitude of gratitude.

9. In what ways does God "oppose the proud" (verse 5)? Have you felt this opposition in your life?

A: Those who are too proud to humble themselves before God and accept Jesus as their Savior will find God's opposition as eternal separation from Him. Even as Christ-followers, our pride can cause us to depend on our own resources or to live in disobedience. He may oppose us by withholding blessings or even allowing painful failures and struggles as a way to soften our proud hearts and turn us back toward Him.

10. Is pride keeping you from heaven? If it is not keeping you from heaven, is it keeping you from a deeper relationship with God and with others? How can this group pray for you?

11. What is one thing you can do in the coming week to clothe yourself with humility?

SESSION 3 — Unravel Anger ... Before It Unravels You

Objectives:
- To recognize how we currently handle our anger
- To adjust our responses so that we don't sin in our anger

1. What memories do you have about anger in your family when you were growing up?

2. Describe a time when a friend or family member made you really mad. What did you do?

Tip: Look for correlations between how anger was modeled in their homes (question 1) and how they handle it now. Often we take our cues from what we see modeled rather than from God's instruction book, the Bible.

3. Which of these examples above most closely describes how you deal with your anger?

   Tip: Be careful not to allow judgment about someone or how they handle anger to enter into the discussion. As the leader, be prepared to guide the conversation away from judgment and toward acceptance and support.

4. Is it selfish or inconsiderate to require others to help you work through your emotions? Why or why not?

   A: We sometimes feel like we have to work through our emotions privately so we don't risk hurting others. It's certainly important not to sin in our anger by over-generalizing (lying) or attacking. But, part of building close relationships is learning how to be honest, expressing the truth in love.

   Tip: There will be a wide range of answers to this question depending on your group. So, don't try to come to a specific conclusion. Your goal is to get folks thinking about how they handle emotions and how they might need to change so they respond more in line with the principles of Scripture.

5. What examples of constructive anger have you seen in others? How can you apply this to your life?

   Tip: Listen as the group discusses their various examples and look for common ground for application in everyone's lives.

6. Does not going to bed angry mean that it is wrong to stop and cool off before confronting a problem? How can we tell when something needs to be thrashed through and when it should be laid to rest for a brief time?

   A: No, it's not wrong to gather your composure and cool off before confronting problems. In fact, problems might escalate if some people do not use this cooling off time. However, there is a time when cooling off becomes putting off. Chewing on our anger for extended periods will only cause it to fester and grow … until it explodes. We need to ask God for wisdom.

7. Can you think of a time when anger carried you past your first emotion of hurt or worry and made you do something mean? In retrospect, how do you think you could have handled this without swinging on the trapeze of anger?

   Tip: A good follow-up question is, "How long did it take for anger to swing you over your first emotions and into something more serious?" Help people recognize the danger of not dealing with their first emotions immediately.

8. Probably most of us are too "civilized" to murder our family members, but that isn't the only sin to which anger leads. What other sins crouch outside the anger door?

    A: The door of anger can swing open to a multitude of sins including slander, adultery, blasphemy, and others.

9. In what situations do you struggle with feelings of anger? How can the group pray for you as you seek to handle this in a God-honoring manner?

10. Is there someone who has hurt you that you need to release right now? What steps do you need to take to initiate reconciliation?

SESSION 4 — Escape the Ugly Green Monster of Envy

Objectives:
- To identify what envy looks like and what results from it
- To identify the steps we can take to move us from envy to contentment

1. When you were in grade school, what did other kids have that made you green with envy?

2. If you got what you wanted, did it live up to your expectations?

    Tip: Follow up by asking if getting this one thing eliminated their envy, or if it just shifted from one thing to another.

3. What kinds of rottenness can envy bring into the lives of people?

    A: Envy can lead to such rotten sins as stealing, cheating, and even murder.

4. Does being content with what we have mean that we should not work to make things better for ourselves? How should we balance ambition and contentment?

    A: Being content doesn't mean shifting life into neutral. It's okay to work hard to improve our lives. The key to balancing ambition with contentment is simply this: rely on Christ to set your goals and to empower change. Don't lean on your own strength, power, or wisdom. Then, you can be content that you are where God wants you ... regardless of the outcome.

5. What is the "secret" of contentment that Paul mentions?

   A: The secret is relying on the power of Christ in you for peace and inner joy, even in the most difficult circumstances. Knowing that God has promised to supply your every need (not necessarily your wants!), and trusting Him to do just that is the only way you can truly find contentment.

6. What are some ways you have seen envy separate you and your peers?

   Tip: This is a question you might want to spend a little extra time on. This type of question can often open some great dialogue as people share their experiences.

7. How are love and envy opposed to one another? How can you reach out with love to those who are separated from you because of envy?

   A: Love and envy repel each other like magnets because of their reversed power sources. Love originates with God. The Bible says "God is love." Envy, however, originates with Satan. Love causes us to reach out to one another; envy drives us to push away as we try to outdo each other.

8. What does it take to feel safe with this level of vulnerability? Do you have someone you could talk to like this?

   Tip: A good follow-up question could be "What fears do we have to overcome to get this close to someone else?"

9. How can you thank God when you don't feel thankful? Is it dishonest to say thanks when you feel the opposite way?

   A: Feelings are fickle. They cannot always be trusted, so not feeling thankful is a poor reason to skip expressing gratitude to God. We thank Him because He deserves it, not because we feel like it.

10. How high on your "pursuit list" is the pursuit of God? If you realize that He is really not number one, what do you think is? Is it really worth it?

    Tip: One way assess this is to look at where we spend our time and money (see Matthew 6:21). Challenge the group to inspect their calendars, checkbooks, and credit card statements, as they prioritize their pursuits.

11. In what areas do you struggle with envy? What will you do in the coming week to overcome it? How can this group pray for you?

    Tip: This is another opportunity for you, as the leader, to set an example by being willing to share an area of struggle.

SESSION 5 — Stop the Sloth from Hanging Around

Objective:
- To understand what slothfulness looks like and how we can stand against it

1. What is your favorite form of relaxation?

2. Do you see yourself as more of a go-getter, or are you a procrastinator? What activities are you most likely to put off until "later"?

   Tip: this question is only an icebreaker, so don't spend too much time on it. But, a good follow-up question is "Why do we tend to procrastinate?"

3. What do you think the different people and things in this parable represent? Why couldn't the wise virgins share their oil with the foolish virgins?

   A: The groom is Jesus and the ten virgins are mankind. The five wise ones represent those of us who are prepared for Christ to come at any time. The five foolish virgins represent those who are unprepared, thinking they know when He will return or that they can prepare at the last minute. The wise virgins could not share their oil because each person had to prepare herself. Likewise, we are each responsible for our own spiritual condition.

4. How can Christ-followers multiply their "talents" for the Master? How might you be burying your talent?

   A: We multiply our talents by investing them in growing Christ's church. If your talent is music, perform for the Lord; if teaching, teach the Word; if hospitality, make others feel welcome; and so on. We bury our talents by ignoring them, denying them, or using them for the wrong purposes.

5. What do these parables tell you about the seriousness of slothfulness?

   A: These parables collectively show that slothfulness is truly a deadly sin. It can cause us to be completely unready for Christ when He returns. It can cause us to waste time and talents He's given us to use during our lives.

6. Can you connect to any of these signs of slothfulness? Give an example of how and where these signs may be evident in your life.

   Tip: Remember to respond with grace as people openly share areas where they need to grow.

7. When Satan looks at you, what areas of vulnerability does he see?

8. What can you actively do to strengthen these areas of weakness?

    A: Strengthen your weaknesses by trusting Christ to provide His super-
        natural strength. When you struggle in an area, try treating that tempta-
        tion as if you are dead to it. How does something that is dead respond?
        It doesn't! The good news is that you are dead to sin IF you know and
        follow Christ. Your sinful self was crucified with Him 2,000 years ago.
        You're now a new creation empowered by the Holy Spirit to have freedom
        from sin's grip. For more on this, see Romans 6:6-7 and Galatians 2:20.

9. What slothful attitudes do you have in your life? Are you slothful in your
    relationships? In recognizing temptation or sin? In serving others? In prayer?

10. What practical action can you take this week to change one of these
    things?

    Tip: Ask the members to be ready to share one way that they "slammed" the
        slothfulness in their lives by the next time you meet together. Don't forget
        to ask about these success stories at your next meeting.

SESSION 6 – Avoid the Lure of Lust

Objective:
  • To recognize the lure of lust and learn lust-busters to help us skip the bait

1. Do you think you are more likely to succumb to a food ad or a "stuff" ad?
    Why?

2. What is an example of an alluring advertisement someone might find tempting?

    Tip: A fun way to address these two questions is to have people bring an
        example of an advertisement that appeals to them. Be sure to specify that
        they need to keep it clean and tasteful ... no nudity or other questionable
        material! Discuss what it is about that ad that gets someone's attention.

3. What could be some of the consequences in your life if you latch on to the
    lure of lust?

    A: Consequences may include marital strife, divorce, damaged relationships
        with children, health risks, career loss, and loss of influence on others.

4. In what way is sexual immorality in particular a sin against one's own body?

    A: The body is owned by God and should be used only as God intends. Sexual sin misuses the body in pursuit of something God detests. When I choose to participate in sexual sin, I am literally choosing to involve a part of me in an activity that will destroy it and turn it away from God.

5. What difference does it make that the Holy Spirit lives in us? What does it look like to honor God with one's body?

    A: As a Christ-follower, the Holy Spirit lives within me. The Bible describes my body as the temple of the Holy Spirit (1 Corinthians 3:16). When I involve my body in sexual sin, I'm dragging along the very home of God.

    Honoring God with our bodies has several implications. Certainly, one is leaving the lure of lust alone and keeping our bodies sexually pure by practicing sex God's way: one man and one woman in a committed marriage relationship. But, this extends beyond sexual activity. Any time we act in obedience to God, we choose to honor Him with our bodies.

6. Select one of these lust-busters and describe some practical ways to live it out in your life.

    Tip: Have someone in the group write the suggestions down. Later, you can take the list and distribute it to all the members for future reference.

7. This verse says that when sin is "full-grown," it gives birth to death. In what way does lust lead to death?

    A: Lust leads to death because it is temptation that tickles our desires to sin, and when sin takes over it eventually leads to the death of some-thing—a relationship, a reputation, future plans, future potential, etc. Even if we don't see them immediately, there are always consequences for sin.

8. The lures of lust are different for men and women. What do men and women need to be aware of in order to be sensitive to the weaknesses of the opposite sex?

    A: Men need to be aware of a woman's desire for an emotional connection. Women should be aware of a man's desires for physical attraction.

9. What does pursuing righteousness look like?

    A: This pursuit requires knowing when to run away from temptation, but also knowing what to run toward. Practically speaking, this means making decisions to follow the Spirit instead of the flesh in daily decisions. It's choosing to pursue God as if He is the most important Person in my life.

10. Do you have collateral damage in your life from the lures of lust? How can this group pray for healing and restoration for you or your family?

11. How can this group help one another to be accountable in this area?

    Tip: Use questions 10 and 11 to lead your group to a time of praise and prayer.

SESSION 7 – Feast on the Good Stuff

Objective:
- To identify the indicators of gluttony and the qualities that we need to develop in our lives to help us resist this sinful distraction

1. As a child, were you a picky eater? What foods did you truly like or dislike?

2. What is one of your favorite foods now?

    Tip: This topic may be very sensitive, especially to those who struggle with being overweight. As you set up this discussion, make sure you point out that gluttony is a problem relevant to everyone, regardless of weight. A thin person who eats to ease his or her pain, can be guilty of this sin. On the other hand, someone with a low metabolism and weight problem who is eating a healthy, balanced diet and depending on God, is not a glutton.

3. In what way could gluttony make one live as an enemy of Christ?

    A: At first glance, this may seem extreme. But the Bible uses the phrase "enemy of Christ" because when we choose to allow something other than God to control us, then we no longer pursue His way. If we are not moving with God, then we are moving against Him. This gives us a perspective on how serious it is when we give the sin of gluttony control in our lives.

4. Who controls your life: God or your physical appetite? How can you tell?

    Tip: Some ways we might be able to tell if our physical appetite is in control:
    - **I eat whenever I am depressed, in a bad mood, or having a rough day.**
    - **Food is the centerpiece of every social event.**
    - **I have the thought, "I know I shouldn't eat this," and eat it anyway.**
    - **I keep eating even when I'm not hungry.**
    - **I struggle to maintain a healthy weight because of my eating habits.**

5. What might "honoring God with your body" look like in the area of food?

    A: Honoring God with our eating habits means keeping a proper perspective about food. We should eat to live, not live to eat. Keeping God first in our priorities honors Him, as does making good food choices as we show respect for the amazing physical bodies He has given us.

6. In what ways could an attitude of gluttony affect other areas of your life?

    A: This kind of self-indulgence paves the way for other areas of indulgence as well, because it is due to a lack of self-discipline. This makes it easier to then be undisciplined when we deal with slothfulness or lust or greed. When we are allowing the Holy Spirit to work in our lives, one of the fruits of that is self-discipline (Galatians 5:22). When the Holy Spirit is producing self-discipline, it will impact every area of our lives, not just gluttony.

7. How are a lack of self-control and a lack of trust in God contributing to the sin of gluttony in your life?

    Tip: Follow up by asking, "What can you do about it?" and "What's the obstacle that's keeping you from doing the right thing?"

8. How does Jesus contrast the manna (a gift from God) and Himself (also from God)? What does this tell us about the importance we should place on physical food?

    A: Jesus said that He is the true bread from heaven and that it is only through Him that a person can have true life. Obviously that places physical food way behind a relationship with Christ on the priority scale.

9. What can we do when the pull of food feels too strong to resist?

    A: Try praying. Ask God to use the Holy Spirit to fill whatever void you are feeling rather than turning to indulgence with food or drink.

10. What place do you think food really plays in your life?

11. What will you do in the coming week to make some "home improvements" for God's temple?

    Tip: Don't let the discussion focus solely on physical fitness. That is important, but remember that gluttony is about attitudes. Consider the answers from question 10 as your group formulates a plan for getting a grip on gluttony.

SESSION 8 — Escape the Grip of Greed

Objective:
- To wrestle free from the grip of greed by developing generosity in our lives

1. Are you more likely to be a "saver" or a "pitcher"? Do you tend to keep junk "just in case it comes in handy someday" or do you throw everything away and go out and buy new stuff when you need it?

2. Are you and your family on the same page with "saving" or "pitching"?

   Tip: For those who are on the same page ask how they got there. For those who are not, ask how they can get there.

3. What does hoarding say about our trust in God? How about generosity?

   A: Hoarding indicates a lack of trust in God to provide for us in the future, plus a lack of realizing His pleasure when we're generous with His stuff.

4. What would "Teflon-getting" look like in your life? Be specific and practical.

   A: For most of us, "Teflon-getting" means giving away stuff as we acquire more. It may mean giving away new stuff or maybe something we've had for a while. It may also involve giving away items we no longer use such as clothing, furniture, appliances, or children's toys. Finally, "Teflon giving" may mean parting with more of our money as God blesses us financially.

5. Read 1 Corinthians 16:1-2. What are the benefits of the method described here of implementing generosity? How might this make it easier to give generously, not grudgingly?

   Tip: A good follow-up question is, "Why is it important to be able to give generously, not grudgingly?"

6. What are some practical ways we can "sow generously"?

   Tip: Keep a list and try to put some of the best ideas into practice as a group.

7. What can we do to change our attitudes and become cheerful, generous givers?

   Tip: Discuss questions 6 and 7 together. Sowing generously and giving cheerfully come from having right attitudes about our money and "stuff."

8. According to these verses, what will the fruits of generosity look like? List some of the results of generous living.

   A: Generosity will produce an attitude of thanksgiving in the ones you are generous with. They will thank God and praise Him for the work He has done through you. When you bless others, you also open the door for God to pour out blessings on you, though this should never be your motivation.

9. If you remained financially at the same level you are now for the rest of your life, would you be content? Would you be joyful? On what do you <u>really</u> base your happiness?

   Tip: This is a difficult question for many people, especially in affluent areas where they are constantly surrounded by materialism and the desire to acquire. Follow up by asking how a person can maintain a proper perspective about their finances and be content with what they have.

10. Where is your focus in life now? How does your relationship with Jesus Christ fit in with your goals and direction?

    Tip: A good follow-up question is, "How can we keep our eyes fixed on Jesus?" Use these last few questions to help you make a list of ways you can pray for each other in the area of greed, as well as other distractions.

11. Which fatal distraction most threatens to lead you off-course? How can this group pray for you?

ACKNOWLEDGMENTS

Creating a small-group study is an amazingly complex task, and is not just one man's effort. I truly appreciate the effective partnership between Fellowship Church and Serendipity House, as well as the individuals who contributed to this effort.

Fellowship Church: Mac Richard contributed the material on gluttony. J.P. Ratigan designed the cover. The Fellowship editorial team included Tianne Moon, Todd Hamilton, and Andy Boyd.

Serendipity House Publishing: Scott Lee developed the interior design and produced the layout. The Serendipity editorial team consisted of Ben Colter, Marilyn Duncan, Katharine Harris, and Cathy Tardif.

Great job team!